Rise of The Young

How To Turn your Negative Situation Into A Positive Outcome and Build a Successful Personal Brand

Casey Adams

Table of Contents

Introduction.. 1

Chapter 1: The Beginning 5

Chapter 2: The Injury 9

Chapter 3: Stuck In A Neck Brace 15

Chapter 4: Investing in Opportunities 31

Chapter 5: The Power of Setbacks 45

Chapter 6: Building a Brand Story 51

Chapter 7: How Successful Entrepreneurs Overcame Negativity....... 77

Chapter 8: Connecting The Dots............................... 113

"I had the opportunity to connect with Casey Adams via Instagram. I was intrigued by his drive, hustle and his influence at a young age. His book has taught me many lessons especially on the power of social media. If you want to grow your brand or business, this book is a must read".

-Michael Alden, USA Today and Wall Street Journal Bestselling author of Ask More Get More and 5% More

"Casey is a rare breed. Despite his young age he's managed to embed himself into top tier events with some of the best speakers in the world & it feels natural that he's sharing the same stage alongside them."

-Dan Fleyshman, youngest owner of a public company, Author of "How to Start Your Business For Under $1,000" and advisor to 26 companies

"Energetic. Authentic. Straight-forward. Casey Adams is a prime example of what millennial entrepreneurs are capable of. Work ethic looks to Casey for its definition."

-Jaiden Gross , 21 Year Old Millionaire Social Media Entrepreneur, Investor, and Business Consultant

Dedicated to my dad, for teaching me the value of hard work

Introduction

Not too long ago I was in my room depressed, not knowing what I wanted to do with my life. I got my passion ripped away from me and I almost became paralyzed. Not knowing what could happen to me had me terrified and I became the most negative version of myself. I could have let the negativity in my life pull me down, but I knew I had to make a massive change in order to see massive results.

At just 16 years old, being in the position of almost getting paralyzed is quite scary. During this time in my life I was headed into my sophomore year of high school and this situation came out of nowhere. In this book I will be explaining to you how I was diagnosed with interspinous ligament damage and how it changed the direction of my life. Also, I will be going over how I was able to turn my negative situation into a positive outcome.

Over the past year and a half since my injury, I've been able to change the direction of my life completely. I've been able to build a well known personal brand on social media, in which I've grown to over 50,000 followers. Also, I've had the opportunity to impact thousands of people with my story and help many individuals see what is possible at a young age. Since my injury, I've been interviewed on ABC Channel 8 News, The Huffington Post, as well as, had the opportunity to speak on stages with many game changing entrepreneurs such as Gerard Adams and Caleb Maddix.

Dealing with such a negative situation led me to searching for ways to overcome it. One of my mentors Tai Lopez helped me redefine what I wanted out of life and overall has helped me go down a different path. I've now had the opportunity to connect with Tai Lopez at his house in Beverly Hills, California in which I'm now a part of his online programs.

In this book I will be sharing with you my story, as well as how I've been able to turn my negative situation into a positive outcome. Not only will you learn how to overcome negativity, I will be sharing with you secrets I've learned about how to connect with such influential individuals. One major thing I've learned from these individuals is the power of networking and how crucial it is to see results.

In the society we live in today, social media gives us the power to network with millions of individuals. Not only will I be sharing with you about how to network on social media, but I will be giving you the secrets on how to build an effective personal brand. Building a personal brand has allowed me to connect with many game changing entrepreneurs and overall has opened up many new opportunities for me. It's time to take action and develop a personal brand that can open up opportunities for you! I'm excited to be going on this journey with you and help you turn your negative situation into a positive outcome.

CHAPTER 1

The Beginning

"Not everybody can be a great entrepreneur, but a great entrepreneur can come from anywhere."

-Gerard Adams

All throughout my life, I've lived in a small county called Chesterfield, Virginia. As a sixteen year old, many people think that having the same group of friends around you twenty-four seven is a blessing. Although having a strong group of friends is important, you must realize when it is time to separate yourself from the people who stop you from levelling up. If you want to see a change in your life, change the people you surround yourself with. Not everybody will have the courage to distance themselves from their so called "friends", but it's those who find the courage to do so that see life changing results. I had the courage to do so, will you?

I've grown up my entire life with a very caring family and they have always supported me in whatever I do. I've grown up with two brothers, one is three years older than me and his name is Cameron. Cameron and I have always had a close relationship and we have always loved competing in whatever we do. As a younger brother, my goal was always to stay on top of my game and overall hang with the older folks. We've competed in activities such as hockey, sprints, basketball, board-games, Xbox Games, Lacrosse, Snowboarding, BMX, Longboarding, skimboarding, surfing and other competitive events. I am telling you this because as I've grown as an individual, I've noticed that the people who want it the most are the ones who get what they want. My older brother Cody is Twenty Two years old and all throughout my life he has been a guide for me. As the older brother, he has always influenced me into what I want to do and has overall helped me figure out when I need to change something. As the younger brother, I have had the ability to analyze what my brothers are doing and see what I have to do different to get a different result. Ever since I was a little kid, I've always had a passion to progress in everything I do. Whether it comes to sports, fitness, selling, games, I've always loved getting better at something I loved. My mom Denise and my dad Kevin have always been supporters in everything I do and they have helped me become the individual I am today. I have no idea where I would be without them, thanks for everything mom and dad.

Find Your Passion

In my own words, passion is the burning desire to do what you want every single day. When I was growing up, I would always find myself outside getting into something new. I was a very optimistic young boy and I always wanted to figure out how things work. With everything I touched, I would want to figure out how to master it. When I was just three years old, I learned how to roller skate and I fell in love with it. The feeling of being able to move freely on wheels always made me so happy and it was an exhilarating experience. As I started skating more frequently, I started being able to skate as fast as both of my brothers. They started playing hockey at a young age and seeing them play hockey motivated me to get on the rink as fast as I could. I remember when I was four years old, I would be playing in games with kids who were eight, nine, and ten years old. The age difference was huge, but as I began to work on my craft I started being able to play with all of them. As the time went on, I started to get more serious about hockey, and it became my biggest passion of all. I progressed in hockey very quickly and I was asked to play for the state of Virginia when I was just eight years old at an event called "State Wars". It was an event in which kids from my state competed with other teams from all over the country. This experience was life changing and it allowed me to showcase my talent and overall compete in a way that I never had before. Competition for me, was always something that got my adrenaline pumping and it allowed me to perform at my best ability. This same type of passion and competitive attitude must be used by you and implemented into your daily life.

Once you find something you are passionate about, you will never want to stop doing what you love. Passion is so important because it allows you to work hard at something you love, but it feels like you're never working. It takes your mind off the stress in your life, and it gives you a feeling of relief on the inside. For me, my passion was sports because it allowed me to progress as an athlete and overall compete with other individuals. Competition is so important, because the energy you build up is something that you cannot replicate outside of a competition. You will always be faced with competition whether it be in sports, business, school, or any other situation that allows you to compete.

All throughout my life, my number one focus has been on sports. It wasn't until freshman year of high school that I started playing football and I never realized how much this sport would create an impact on my life. I was going into sophomore year of high school and something happened to me that changed the direction of my life forever.

CHAPTER 2

The Injury

"Life is 10 precent what happens to you and 90 percent how you react to it."

- Charles R. Swindoll

When I was a freshman in high school I played football for my school, but I didn't get a lot of playing time the very first year, and I knew I had to change. I started putting in the extra work, coming in before practice started and staying late every single day. At my high school known as Manchester High School, our football team practices from January until September. As freshman year came to a close, I knew that I had to continue to work hard so that I could earn a starting position sophomore year. Little did I know that everything would change....

As football was starting up again sophomore year, I was determined to land a starting position on my football team. I had worked hard every single day since freshman year ended and I was ready to go all in. As sophomore year weight lifting started in January, I was worked hard to prepare for the season. Our team did weight lifting from January until August and then the real practices would start. As we practiced throughout the year, I spoke with many coaches and they told me that I would be starting as a wide receiver. I was very excited for the season, and I was ready to make big plays. As July came to an end, everybody was getting pumped up for August practice because that is when we put on the pads, and started getting ready for our first game. It was an exciting time of year, and everybody on the team had a positive flow of energy because the season was right around the corner.

On August 1st, 2015 it was the first day of hitting practice for our team. Everybody was at the field by 6am, and we were all ready to start tearing up the field. As we all are putting on our pads in the locker room, some teammates headed down to the field so that we could start our first drill. Little did I know that it would be the last time I put on a pair of football pads ever again. The first day of hitting practice consisted a lot of checking equipment such as the shoulder pads and the helmets of all the players. The equipment check was to make sure that everybody was safe to start getting physical. Our first drill was called the B drill and it consisted of two players going against each other one vs. one. The thrilling part about this drill is that the entire team would make a circle around the individuals who were going up against each other. This made the drill very active, and the entire team would be getting hyped up. The drill starts off by choosing two players that are about the same size and they set up five feet apart, put one hand on the ground, get into a football position and go at it. When you hear the whistle go off, your goal is to take your opponent to the ground.

As I'm watching everybody do the drill, I'm getting pumped up because I know it was the year that I was going to shine on the field. As a team, we had been practicing our routes for weeks now, running plays, weight lifting, doing sprints daily, and I was feeling very good about the season. Next, I heard my name get called and it was my turn to do the drill. As I'm approaching the middle of the circle I got ready and everybody gathered around watching. I got down on one arm and I get into a football position not knowing that this would be a major turning point in my life. I heard the whistle blow and I exploded from the line with everything in me. As we came hurdling at each other from 5 yards apart, my opponent and me smash into each other and everybody is hyped up. After about five seconds I began to get a better grip on my opponent and I thought to myself that I was going to win this drill. I begin pushing him backwards and I started to take him down due to the loss of his balance.

As I fell on top of him, about to take him to the ground, he used his strength to try and spin me so that I would end up landing on my back. While we were falling down to the ground, he ended up being able to transition me from being on top, to hit the ground with my back. In this split second of time in the air, he spun me so fast that it ended up causing my chin strap to slide off my chin and come up past my nose. The sudden movement caused my chin strap to be positioned past my nose and made it so my helmet was tilted back touching my spine.

My neck ended up taking all of the impact of his weight, in which my helmet was directly positioned in between one of my vertebrates. My head slammed on the ground with extreme force and I immediately felt a burning sensation in my neck/spine. As the play came to an end, I lay there for a moment trying to comprehend what has just happened. I struggled getting up due to the fact that my helmet was half way off my face, but I finally stood up and started walking to the side of the field. During that moment I had no idea what had just happened, but I did know that while I hit the ground my helmet was positioned on my spine. As I walk over to the side of the field I start turning my head to the left and to the right trying to get this burning pain out of my neck. I started massaging the spot in which the pain was, but nothing is helping. I knew that I needed to sit out for a little while due to the tingling in my neck, so I told my coaches that I needed a break due to what had just happened during the drill.

After fifteen minutes of sitting on the sideline, the pain has not gone down at all. I spoke to my coaches and told them what happened, and I notified them that I would not be able to go back into practice for the rest of the day. During that moment in time, I thought nothing bad of the situation except the fact that my neck was hurting very badly. I had a strong feeling that everything was going to be okay, but that is not what happened at all.

CHAPTER 3

Stuck In A Neck Brace

"Do not dwell on the past. Your history cannot be erased, but your future has yet to be written, so make the most of what is going to happen instead of worrying about what you cannot change."

-anonymous

As I woke up the following morning, I lay there in my bed not being able to move my neck. I sat up very frantically and as I tried to move my head left and right I felt a very sharp pain. My neck was very stiff and I knew that something wasn't right. I began to inform my mom about what happened yesterday at practice and I told her that I wanted to go get it checked out by a doctor. She agreed with the idea due to the fact that she noticed I could barely move my neck at all. We went to the doctor that morning, not knowing that the outcome would be life changing.

My mindset at that moment was very positive, in that I believed that it was just going to be a small injury. I waited patiently in the waiting room, but after about twenty minutes the doctor came out and called my name. Slowly, I walked back to the room that he directed me to and I began to tell the doctor what happened at practice. The doctor started asking me questions regarding where the pain was occurring and I told him exactly what it felt like. To me it felt like a stabbing sensation in my spine and it was restricting me from being able to move my neck.

After getting analyzed by the doctor, he suggested that I get an X-ray so that they could see if there was any significant damage. As I waited patiently in the room, a nurse came in and directed me towards the X-ray room. We ended up taking eight X-rays in many different positions because the doctor wanted to see my spine from many different angles. After we finished doing the X-rays, the nurse told me that the doctors would be reviewing my X-rays and that they would be with me shortly. She sent me back to the room in which my mom was waiting patiently and we both sat there and waited for the results.

After sitting in the room for ten minutes with my mom, we finally heard a knock on the door. As the door slowly opened the doctor walked in, but he did not have a good look on his face. He shut the door behind him, and sat down in the chair located at the computer. Then, he politely told my mom and I to come closer to the screen so that he can discuss what had happened to my neck. We both gathered around his computer eager to hear the news, but we had no idea what was coming. Slowly, he began pointing to the screen of his computer and had a strange look on his face. Next, he told me that when I hit my head on the ground my helmet had "guillotined" my spine and that I had a concussion. That wasn't only it, he pointed to a specific point on my spine and told me that I had been diagnosed with Interspinous Ligament Damage.

What Is The Interspinous Ligament?

The interspinous ligaments play the purpose of connecting spinous processes of the vertebra to the spine, in which are made up of thin and membranous substances.

My thoughts

During that moment I had no idea what to think, but I knew it did not sound good. My mom looked at the doctor with a puzzled look on her face, and began to ask the doctor many questions. She asked:

- What does this mean?

- Will he be okay?

- How does he recover from this?

- Will he be able to practice again soon?

- How will this affect his season?

As my mom is asking the doctor all of these questions, the doctor stops her. I'm sitting there waiting to hear what I have to do to get better. All I can think about is getting back on that field, but the news did not sound good at all.

THE BAD NEWS

The impact that my helmet had on my spine was very severe. According to the X-ray, the doctor told me that my neck was massively unstable. This meant that I had little to no movement in my neck and that there was a high possibility that it could remain this way for the rest of my life. Also, the doctor informed me that this type of injury had the capability to paralyze me from the neck down. Due to the positioning of my helmet, I did not get paralyzed, but he informed me that it could have been a likely outcome. As I am heard all of this information, he informed me that there is a high possibility that I would never be able to play contact sports again.

To make things worse, the doctor leaves the room for a moment and comes back with an outrageous looking contraption that happens to be a neck brace. It turned out that my neck was so unstable that it needed to be in a neck brace for over ten weeks. He unpackaged the neck brace and told me that I had to wear it at all times besides in the shower. This meant that I had to sleep in a neck brace that restricted me from moving my head at all and I was required to keep it on until I gained mobility in my spine. He placed the neck brace around my neck and I instantly felt restricted from life. At this point I was speechless, everything on the inside of me went numb and I was lost for words.

THE REACTION

As an individual who has never experienced a serious injury, this caused my mind to go blank. My eyes were staring into space as I was trying to process what the doctor told me. Hearing that this injury could have caused me to be paralyzed caught me off guard. The most breathtaking part of the conversation was when he said that I might never be able to play contact sports again. I walked into that room thinking that I was going to be fine and then everything changed so quickly. My mother and I walked out of the doctors' office in utter silence. She knew how passionate I was about football and she had no idea how to respond to what just happened. This was a life changing moment for me and it put in perspective how fast things can change.

PULLED AWAY FROM MY PASSION

Things in my life began to change so quickly. I went from being passionate about playing football everyday to lying in my room not being able to move my neck. I've been working for the last two years on getting better at football and it was finally my time to shine. The unexpected happened and suddenly I was never able to play football again. My passion was taken away from me so quickly and I couldn't do anything about it.

Depressed Situation

From that point forward I became so depressed. Day by day, I woke up in my neck brace unable to move and the rest of my team was continuing to get ready for the season. Every minute that I was in that neck brace I was dwelling on the situation. I became the most negative version of myself and fell into a very dark place. The anger on the inside of me would be expressed towards everybody I spoke to. The situation changed me and the people around me began to notice. My mom and dad began to notice how depressed I was getting and continuously tried to cheer me up. Nothing worked, each and everyday the same thoughts would flow through my head. Instead of focusing on how I was going to get better, I was getting suffocated by the negativity.

Everything changed so fast and I had never thought that a situation like this could happen to me. I went from being in a mindset of happiness and excitement for the season and in a matter of twenty four hours my life had changed forever. My passion for football was instantly torn away from me and my mindset about life was put into a negative atmosphere.

Weeks went by and I continued to live in this negative mindset. I felt that I had no purpose in life anymore and that everything that I had been working towards was a waste of time. School was approaching and I had no motivation to do anything because of my lack of purpose. My team was getting close to their first game and I was getting closer to my first day of physical therapy.

This is not how I had expected my sophomore year to start, but there was nothing I could do about the situation. While I was in my neck brace an average day for me consisted of lying in bed, being on my phone and watching movies.

From depressed to obsessed

One day while I was lying in my bed I ran across a video that changed my perspective on life. It was a video of Tai Lopez (@tailopez), and he was talking about how he could help transform all aspects of your life including your health, wealth, love and happiness. For those who don't know who Tai Lopez is, he is an Investor/Advisor to over 20 multi-million dollar companies. Also, he owns one of the world's largest book clubs with over 1.4 million people in over 40 different countries. Tai's video intrigued me and I was very tuned into what he had to say. The way he was telling his story connected with me because he was talking about the negative times in his life. After weeks of pure negativity in my life, this video triggered something in my mind that caused me to deeply think about my situation. In Tai's video he talked about what he learned from his mentors and how much of an impact reading had on his life. At the time I did not read a lot, but Tai caught my attention and I wanted to learn more.

Injured spine to 67 steps

After watching Tai's video he offered the opportunity to get into his 67 step program. At the time $67 was a lot of money for me to invest, but I had a feeling that his program could help me in my current situation. I read over some testimonials that Tai had on the page and many people were finding his content very valuable. The situation I was in was very lethal and the more I continued to be negative the worse it got. My intuition told me that I needed to make the investment into myself. I instantly took action and was ready to see what the course had to offer me.

NEW DAILY HABITS

Before I got into Tai's 67 step course, I didn't know what to expect due to the fact that I have never bought a program like his online. The main focus of the 67 steps according to Tai was to help you find the good life in all pillars of your life including health, wealth, love, and happiness. In my situation I was depressed and couldn't physically move around a lot, causing my happiness to be at an all time low.

Once I started the course, I began watching the introduction video that explained to me what the course was going to cover. The 67 steps is a 67 day course that is created to help you rewire your brain, and create new habits in your life. He began to explain the big picture of the course, and overall gave me an in depth review before I got started. Tai spoke about how powerful mentors were to him and at the time I did not understand his thinking. The complexity of his thinking sparked a strong interest into me and I was instantly glued to his video. The introduction video consisted of him talking about:

• Real life changes

• How it takes 67 days to form new habits

• The gradual rise to success

• "The good life"- Health, wealth, love and happiness

- The importance of reading

- The value of investing in yourself

- RRD items (Rust, Rot, Depreciate)

- Paralysis of analysis

- Mental frameworks of the brain

At the time, all of what he was talking about sounded foreign. I was not brought up in a place where reading was pressed upon me nor was I introduced to success principles. The knowledge I gained from the first introduction video was of immense value and I was ready to be consistent with the course.

A video a day helped me find my way

Once I purchased the course, I had a burning desire to finish it. Ever since watching the first video, I was hooked and ready to take action. Now that I look back on Tai's 67 step course, I see how it opened up my life to new opportunities. What he teaches you inside the course is mindset shifts that keep you ahead of the game. The videos are very compelling and ever since I got into the program I have looked at the world with a new perspective.

I began watching a video a day and while I would watch the videos I would take in depth notes. The knowledge of each video was so much for me to comprehend, but Tai did a great job of explaining each principle. The great thing about the course is it gave me practical ways to apply each principle to my life. As I continued to go through his program, I began to adapt a more positive mindset. It wasn't an overnight shift, but the principles he was instilling in my head began to affect my emotions. The out pouring of knowledge from his mentors cultivated into my daily life and it started to give me hope while I was sitting at home not knowing what to do. Watching a video a day started to become a daily habit and I started implementing what I was learning in the course. For example, Tai spoke about the power of books. Before I got into the 67 steps I did not read at all, but as he began to instil this knowledge into my brain I started getting curious to how much books could affect my life. He spoke about how the majority of the world's billionaires all had a library at their houses. This led me to thinking if I wanted to get out of this negative stage in my life, I must begin to act like the top 1%. Tai began recommending books I should read and I instantly began to take action.

Shortly after getting into Tai's program I started building new daily habits. I started reading more and the energy I began to get while listening to him was unreal. The fundamental principles I started learning sparked a fire inside of me and I began to feel energized on a daily basis. Remember, during this time I was still in my neck brace and for me to say I was starting to be positive was a huge step for me.

Building new daily habits was a vital step I took in order to help overcome my negative situation. Once I began to rewire my brain and implement new habits on a daily basis I started to feel like a whole new person. You must focus on doing activities that will help build you towards your goals. One of the biggest takeaways I got from Tai was to look at your life as a sculpture, meaning that you must chip away at it every single day. Many people expect significant changes to happen overnight, but do not come to the realization that significant changes happen over time. Chip away at your life everyday and focus on getting closer to your goals. If you are spending most of your time on tasks that are not helping you get out of your negative situation, then you must change your daily habits. Your habits determine what you do on a daily basis and what you do on a daily basis defines who you are. Learning from Tai Lopez was the best investment I've ever made into myself, and it was the pivot point in my life that helped me overcome my negative situation.

(Learn more at www.tailopez.com/67steps)

Neck brace to New Mindset

When I got put into my neck brace I became the most negative version of myself. I had no idea what I was supposed to do and I hated what my life had come to. I was dwelling on the negative situation and didn't realize that something so small could make such a huge difference in my life. I learned during my injury that your life can change so quickly and you must be grateful for every moment you have on this earth. In order for me to overcome this situation, I began self educating myself and rewiring my brain. The habits that I built up inside of my brain positioned me on a path of optimism and overall helped me develop self confidence during my negative time. Once you build a mindset of self confidence, your negative energy will soon dwindle. Those who are in a negative situation in their life have the resources to change their life. We live in a world filled with free information including audio books, YouTube, online courses and much more. Start by developing fundamental habits that will benefit you on a daily basis and you will start to see changes. Not everybody will have the willpower to find what will benefit them, but the ones who do will be greatly benefitted. The best investment you can ever make is into yourself. People who have the courage to solve problems, and search for their answers will be rewarded the best. I was in a negative mindset and I had a gut feeling that the 67 step course would help me. I had no idea what I was getting myself involved in, but later on down the road I learned that the course caused me to overcome my injury. Your mindset will define what you do on a daily basis and what you do on a daily basis will defines who you are as an individual. Develop a mindset that will allow yourself to overcome your negative situation and stick to your plan. No matter your situation, you can always look for the positive side of things. Focus on sucking the negativity out of yourself by surrounding yourself with positive people who move you forward. Overall, you must learn to adapt to each situation that occurs in your life. Instead of focusing on the negative, invest into new daily habits and change your mindset.

What can I do to get out of my negative situation?

- Invest into yourself

- Focus on your outcome, and not your current situation

- Have faith in what you are doing

- Stop complaining, and go do something about it

- Stop sitting back, and focus on building new relationships

- Actively educate yourself

During this stage in my life when I started to see a change in my mindset, I began realizing that it was due to the fact that I changed my daily actions. Before my injury all I focused on was getting better at football and I rarely ever focused on personal development. I was stuck in a cycle in which I would hang out with the same group of friends and I was getting the same results. Going through this negative situation in my life opened my eyes to the fact that things can change so quickly. You as an individual must realize that your situation can change massively in the course of a single day. I woke up on that morning of hitting practice not knowing that it would cause me to go down a completely different path. The injury put me into realization that change is inevitable and you as an individual must be ready for whatever life throws at you. Your ability to reposition yourself to any given situation will allow you to stay positive and overall dominate any situation. At first it seemed impossible to become positive after suffering from an injury like mine. It dragged me into the darkest hole, but I did not let my situation define who I am. You must remember that life is 10% what happens to you, and 90% how you react. As an individual, many negative situations are going to appear in your life but you cannot let them define who you are. Change your daily habits and learn to rewire your brain for the better. Remember, not everybody will have the courage to overcome their negative situation, but it's those who do that become the most fulfilled individuals.

CHAPTER 4

Investing in Opportunities

Life's up and downs provide windows of opportunity to determine your
values and goals. Think of using all obstacles as stepping stones to build
the life you want.

-Marsha Sinetar

E very single day that you wake up, you invest in opportunities. You must start coming to the realization that no matter what you're doing, you are investing. Whether it be investing your time, energy, or money, you always are sacrificing one of those 3 pillars for something in return. Time is a finite object and you must utilize your time to the fullest each and every day. You only get 24 hours per day on this planet and you must focus on how you are using them. Every multi millionaire/billionaire has the same amount of time per day, but they have found out how to properly utilize their time. There is so much opportunity all around you, but it is not just going to pop out at you. In order to get what you want, you must search for what you want. So many people are expecting changes in their life, but they aren't doing anything to change. To uncover the opportunities within you, you must step out of your comfort zone. Connect with new individuals because you never know the direction in which one person can lead you.

Tai Lopez spoke a lot about mentors in his course, and he inspired me to go out and search for a multitude of individuals. One key point I took from his course is that in order to experience an immense learning curve, you must learn from other successful individuals. Investing your time into other people will allow you to gain the knowledge that they have compiled over their entire life. You must look at your time as the most valuable asset you have because it is a finite object. You can not get time back, nor can you get this exact moment in your life back. The opportunities that are available to you today will not be available forever, so you must learn to take action now. This exact moment in your life will never be the same, so you must begin to realize how important it is to invest in every opportunity you can.

When I got started into affiliate marketing, I took a risk and invested into a product that allowed me to help people build capture pages for their business. Before I took action on this new business venture, my mom made me sign up for two jobs at a local restaurant near me. Fortunately, I ended up not getting the jobs due to the fact that the restaurants were already over staffed. As an individual, I did not want to get a normal day job and I saw it as an opportunity for me to invest into an online business. The system is called Online Sales Pro and when I got started I had never done any sort of online marketing in my life. When I first started using the system, I was able to generate over 60 sales in the first month alone by using Snapchat. Many people ask me, "How did you leverage Snapchat to make sales?" and it all comes down to one simple ideology.

"No matter what business you are in, you are always in the people business"

-Casey Adams

The point of me telling you how I made 60 sales using Snapchat is based around the lesson it has taught me. When I first got started, I saw many people trying to sell the system by annoying another individual. People would literally message others telling them to buy a product when they have never even spoken to that person in their life. To me that was not how it was suppose to work, and I started using methods that I have learned from Grant Cardone. One lesson that I used was to build a relationship with the individual I was speaking to, and solve their problem using my system. I would personally connect with everybody that was following me and send them a personal message asking them about what they do. This gave me an advantage over others because I knew who I was talking to and it helped me figure out how I can help them to the best of my ability. Remember, no matter what you are doing in your life, you are always going to build relationships with people. For me it was simple, I leveraged Snapchat by building relationships with people and found out how my product could solve their problem. Once you can solve somebody's problem, you can provide so much value to that individual. In whatever you are doing in life, start focusing on the value you are providing to people. I've learned at a young age that building connections is a very important aspect to your success and I want you to start focusing on building relationships with the people you interact with.

Taking a risk and getting involved with this opportunity has opened up so many doors in my life. It's allowed me to connect with multiple game changers and has overall taught me a valuable lesson about the power of building relationships. This is a lesson that I am so thankful for because it applies to every aspect of my life. No matter what you are doing right now in your life, building strong relationships and connecting with others will open up so many doors for you.

Opportunity doesn't last forever

As an individual, you must start to put yourself in positions to be faced with new opportunity. The quickest way you can be introduced to new opportunities is by surrounding yourself with new people. The more people you network with, the more ways you can help other people. You must get yourself out there and build your network. The people you meet in the next 6 to 12 months will dictate the path you go down in your life. If you surround yourself with negative people who are pessimistic, it is likely that you will not be faced with much opportunity. The people who are negative about life receive negative outcomes. You are the sum of the five people you hang around, so make sure you take a moment right now to think about who you surround yourself with on a daily basis. In order for you to be introduced to new opportunities in your life, you must change what you do on a daily basis. The quicker you change your daily actions, the faster new opportunities will come your way.

Simply by changing my daily actions and connecting with new individuals I have been able to transform my life. At first I did not know how much opportunity was waiting for me, but I took action on what I believed was right. There will never be a "perfect" time to make a change in your life, you must believe in your intuition and take action.

*"You can't **connect** the **dots** looking forward; you can only **connect** them looking backwards. So you have to trust that the **dots** will somehow **connect** in your future. You have to trust in something — your gut, destiny, life, karma, whatever."*

-Steve Jobs

Focus on where you want to go

The people who you hang around are the exact correlation on where you are headed. In order for you to overcome a negative situation, or be introduced to new opportunities you must focus on your outcome. Many people I know wake up every single day and have no goals they want to achieve. They wake up everyday and have absolutely no idea on what they want to do, or where they want to go. It is important that you begin thinking about where you want to be in the next five to ten years. This will allow you to have an end destination in mind, allowing you to map out what you must accomplish to get there. Yes it's important to have an end goal in mind, but you must begin to double down on what you do on a daily basis. No significant changes are going to happen overnight, but the sum of the daily actions you take will lead towards your outcome.

A huge inspiration to me has been fifteen year old Caleb Maddix. He has written over six books at just fifteen and he made his first $100,000 by the age of fourteen. He has spoken all over the world with leaders such as Tony Robbins, Gary Vaynerchuck, Kevin Harrington, Gerard Adams and many more.

I've had the opportunity to connect with Caleb in San Diego, California because he invited me out to speak at an event with him. I will go over that story later in the book, but there is one quote from Caleb Maddix that I want to share with you right now.

"Information plus application equals transformation."

-Caleb Maddix

A lot of people spend a lot of time reading books, attending seminars, listening to podcasts, but they never take action. Don't get me wrong, all of those things are important to grow as an individual, but action is what will transform your life. There is a lot of valuable information out there in the world for free, but without application you will never see a transformation in your life. Caleb Maddix didn't make $100,000 by the age of fourteen by sitting at home doing nothing, HE TOOK MASSIVE ACTION. Focus on developing an actionable plan that you can follow each and every day when you wake up.

Over the past couple of months Caleb Maddix and I have built a relationship and he is about to drop some value for you right now. Make sure you take what he says, and implement it into your life.

Words From Caleb Maddix

Yo! What's up guys! How cool is this? I get to feature in Casey's book!

First off... you guys are extremely lucky to have this book in your hands. I know you guys have already gotten extreme value. Casey Adams is a legit guy who is making extreme moves! Glad to call him a friend.

I just wanted to stop in and write a page or two basically to tell you guys the following.

My entire life, I have practiced the habit of writing out my goals. Every morning since about 9 years old, I have written on a piece of paper, the things I want to accomplish and when I want to accomplish them by.

At 12 years old, I had a goal that went like this, "I am gonna write a book at 20 years old." And I wrote this out every single day. One day, I was writing out that goal and right about halfway through me writing it... I stopped and had a crazy thought. What if I stop saying I am "gonna" write a book, and I do it now!

So I started brainstorming and doing research on how to write a book. And guess what... within 2 months, I finished the book and had it in my hands! The book was called "Keys To Success For Kids!"

Since then, the book has gone across the world and thousands of people have bought it! I have been in other countries and people have walked up to me and told me they read my book!

Not only that… but the book led me to be on national television in front of 8 million people. I have also been featured in Forbes, Huffington Post, Entrepreneur Magazine, Success Magazine, and Inc Magazine! I was voted in the Top 20 Most Motivational People On The Planet & The Top 30 Entrepreneurs Under 30.

I have also connected with insane influencers like CASEY ADAMS, Gary Vaynerchuk, Tony Robbins, Jake Paul, Grant Cardone, Darren Hardy, Kevin Harrington, and many more.

Not to mention… I have written 5 other books since then and I write a book a month! I also own multiple companies including Mentored By Maddix.

I have had dozens of viral videos and reach over 10 million people a week on social media.

I have helped hundreds of other kids write their own books, start their own businesses, make thousands of dollars, and some kids have not committed suicide who were going to, because of my work!

And I have made hundreds of thousands of dollars doing what I love!

I am not telling you all this to show off… I am telling you this to show you what is possible if you stop saying you are "gonna."

The gun that kills the most people is the "gonna." Most people's dreams are killed because they always say they're going to do stuff but they never actually do them! The day I stopped saying I was gonna write a book and instead, I actually did... that's the day my life changed forever.

So whatever goal you have, whatever vision, go after it today! There are seven days in a week, someday is not one of them!

So, if you want to dream... take a nap... but if you want to succeed... wake up and work your face off!

Thanks Casey Adams for letting me write something quick in your book! Excited to see this thing become a best seller! You are killing it!

PS - The information in this book will not transform your life because information doesn't equal transformation. Information plus application equals transformation! So apply what Casey is saying, and go do great things!

Follow Caleb Maddix on Instagram

Instagram: @calebmaddix

If you haven't already followed Caleb Maddix on Instagram, then make sure you do! Caleb just dropped massive value on you, and he does that on an everyday basis on social media. I am honored to have Caleb as a good friend of mine, and so grateful to have him in my book. Make sure you implement what he is saying, and take action today. Massive results come from massive action, but it all starts with you. Learn from this 15 year old who is crushing it, and make a change in your life today. Stop saying you are "gonna" do something, and take action on it today.

Use your M.I.N.D

Look at it like this, if you have the fastest car in the world sitting in your garage, but no gas in the car, you will never get anywhere. You may have a brilliant idea, or a vision on how you are going to execute your idea, but the one thing you may be missing is action. Action is the fuel to the car (you), and without it you won't get anywhere.

One of the quotes that I say is, "use your MIND," and what I mean by that is,

M - mentally

I - identify

N - new

D - directions

In order for you to start seeing new opportunities in your life, you must identify where you want to go. You must construct a mental map in your head of where you are heading, and how you are going to get there. Identify new directions for yourself, and take action on that plan. Come to the conclusion that without a direction, there is no destination. Many individuals in society today get "comfortable" with their situation even though they may hate it. They slave away at a job they hate, and consistently do the exact same thing on a daily basis. People who lack the ability to strive for growth will never reach their full potential. It's up to you to identify where you want to go, and only you have the ability to make it happen.

Ignore the distractions, take action

As you begin to gain clarity on the direction you want to take your life, you must begin to cut out the people who will stop you from levelling up. For me this was hard because I've had the same group of friends since middle school. Once I came to the conclusion that the group of people I was hanging around were limiting me to my full potential, I instantly disregarded them from my life. Not only will the people you surround yourself with have a direct correlation of your outcome, but the information you take into your brain on a daily basis will impact your results. You must ignore all of the irrelevant distractions in your life, and begin to take action on what matters. Surround yourself with people who have faith in your goals, and are willing to motivate you. Many distractions will come up in your life, but you must focus on where you want to go. Each and every day is another opportunity for you to take action on your goals. Investing time into yourself will give you the ability to open new doors of opportunity. There will never be an exact path for you, but as you continue on your journey you will start to gain clarity on where you want to go.

In order for you to overcome your negative situation, you must begin to take action. When I say take action I mean for you to go change something about your situation. Those who go out and get out of their comfort zone will start to see changes in their life. You must be willing to sacrifice something you've been doing forever, and replace it with a new habit. You will be faced with many people who will tell you to just "wait" for things to get better. This mentality will eliminate you from seeing massive changes, and overall keep you at the level that you are currently at. Distractions will cause you to lose focus, and they will hold you back from your full potential. Stay clear on what you want to get done, and focus on surrounding yourself with people who will help you reach your goals.

CHAPTER 5

The Power of Setbacks

"Twenty years from now, you will be more disappointed by the things that you didn't do than by the ones you did do. So throw off the bowlines. Sail away from the safe harbor. Catch the trade winds in your sails. Explore. Dream. Discover."

-Mark Twain

Many people tend to face setbacks in their life that blind them from reality. There are situations that you are going to face, in which you feel like nothing's going your way. Many people let their negative situation define who they are, and what they are going to accomplish. You must adapt a new mindset, and start looking at your setbacks in a positive perspective. One of the world's most powerful teens once said, *"your setbacks, are 'set up' for your comebacks."*

-Caleb Maddix.

As you begin making an effort to turn your negative situation into a positive outcome, you must remember a few things:

- Focus on where you want to be

- Take action on your goals

- Cut out the negative people in your life

- Invest in opportunities

The fundamental principles that I listed above will play a huge part in discovering the power of your setback. First, when you get introduced to a negative situation in your life you begin to look at life in a different perspective. Situations such as an injury, a divorce in your family, a death, getting in trouble with the law, or financial issues will cause you to be in a negative state of mind. Your inner feelings reflect what is happening on the outside, and you are the only person who has the power to change your mindset. When I first got diagnosed with interspinous ligament damage, I had so much negative vibrations in my mind. This caused me to become angry at people, and overall it changed the way I behaved. I did not begin to see improvement in my situation until I started compiling new information into my brain. I began reading a lot more, and this caused me to see a gradual change in my thinking. Not everybody can benefit from reading, and some people may hate reading. As an individual you must identify what works best for you, and take action on it immediately.

A transition of thinking

When a negative situation appears in your life, it will cause you to think in a new way. In order for you to start thinking better of your situation, you must begin to implement a transition of your thinking. Instead of dwelling on what is happening, start focusing on where you want to be and how you are going to get there. A lot of people let their vision of themselves limit them from achieving what they are capable of. For you to start getting real results, you must first believe that you can do something. Once you develop faith in overcoming your situation, you will begin to attract your ideal outcome. You must be willing to do whatever it takes to overcome your negative situation, and overall develop a mindset that will allow you to push yourself forward.

Five ways to change your way of thinking:

1. Be outcome oriented

2. Believe in yourself

3. Alter your daily actions

4. Think big

5. Take massive action

Why setbacks are important

In order for you to grow as an individual, you must experience change. Not just temporary change, but massive change that leaves an impact on you. For me, my massive change was being diagnosed with interspinous ligament damage. When the situation was happening I did not think positive at all, but as I began getting into personal development I began to realize how important setbacks are. A setback is an important aspect of your life because they define who you are as an individual. Also, a setback helps you mentally identify what you don't want to happen, therefore, you can reverse engineer your situation and focus on improving your outcome. You may be going through a difficult time right now, but you must understand that it defines who you are. Nobody else in the entire world has the same story as you, embrace it.

Setbacks = Comebacks

While I was going through my negative situation I had no idea that my setback would have such a huge impact on my life. As I look back I have gained a huge perspective on the power of a negative situation. Once you reach an all time low in your life, you begin looking for a way out. I was in a very dark place once I tore the ligament in my spine because I knew that I could never play football ever again. Now that I look back on my situation, I have come to the realization that my injury is what fuelled me to go after bigger goals. Once I had my passion completely pulled away from me I began intensively searching for another way to be fulfilled. During that time I would have never imagined that my injury would lead me into so many opportunities. You must be optimistic about your future, and use the negativity in your life as fuel for greatness.

As you are reading this section of the book, there are two ways that you can implement this lesson. You can either start looking at your negative situation as fuel for your greatness, or you can sit back and remain negative. Yes, it is going to be hard to overcome a major setback in your life, but there is no growth in the comfort zone. I strongly believe that everything in life happens for a reason, and that each situation will correlate back into a desired outcome. You may be confused right now in your current situation, but as you continue along your journey you will start to gain clarity. For me it took almost getting paralyzed to gain clarity on the direction I want to take my life. During that time it was the worst thing that has ever happened to me, but as I look back I realize that it was meant to happen. The perspective I gained on life was so surreal, and I began to realize that life is so delicate.

You must start looking at every moment in your life as an opportunity for you to progress. Focus on being a better person than you were yesterday, and you will begin to see massive changes.

The Bow and Arrow Effect

In order for a bow to launch an arrow through the air at high speeds, it must be pulled back. You must start looking at the negative situations in your life like a bow and arrow. In your current situation you may be feeling like nothing is going your way, or that you are very unlucky. You must cut out this mental framework, and start looking at your situation as an opportunity for you to come back even better. Start seeing your negativity as a powerful tool for you to accomplish great things. As you feel you are getting pulled back in life, imagine that you are the arrow about to launch into greatness. This will give you a whole different outlook on your life, and with this new mindset you will start turning your negative situation into a positive outcome.

CHAPTER 6

Building a Brand Story

"It's important to build a personal brand because it's the only thing you're going to have. Your reputation online, and in the new business world is pretty much the game, so you've got to be a good person. You can't hide anything, and more importantly, you've got to be out there at some level."

– Gary Vaynerchuk

As an individual you must start to realize that in today's world there is more opportunity than ever before. Many people including myself have been through a negative time in their life, but not everybody has the ability to transform their situation. People are blinded about how they can turn their mess into their message, and create something massive out of it. I've been able to use the power of social media to transform my situation, and overall create so many life changing opportunities for myself. In today's world you must understand that people are connected to stories. Social media has given you the opportunity to craft a personal brand, and tell your story to the world. You may not see it now, but by building a well known personal brand, you are able to unlock many new opportunities in your life.

By using the power of social media to create a brand story, I've been able to completely change my situation at just 16 years old. Not only have I built a massive following on social media with over 50,000 followers, but I've been able to open up many doors of opportunity by utilizing my personal brand. I have been able to tell my story on ABC Channel 8 news, The Huffington Post, as well as speak on stage with many successful entrepreneurs such as Gerard Adams, Caleb Maddix, and many more. Also, I've created the opportunity to be flown out to Beverly Hills, California to meet with Tai Lopez, and feature in some of his online training programs. Now, this didn't happen overnight, and of course it took a lot of work, but I know that you have the ability to create a well known personal brand that can create many new opportunities for yourself.

Leveraging Social Media To Tell Your Story

Weather you've had a very negative situation happen in your life or not, everybody still has their own story. The difference is, not everybody is using the tools we have today to express their story, and overall make a difference on the world. Over the course of the last 18 months I've been able to impact thousands of people by leveraging social media to tell my story. Not only have I been able to impact many lives, but I've been able to travel all over the world telling my story. Every since I started using social media to build a personal brand I've seen many new opportunities come into my life. In this chapter I will be going over ways that you can start to use social media to create a brand story for yourself, and open up many new opportunities for yourself.

I dealt with a very negative situation in my life, and during the time of my injury I was very depressed and had no direction for my life. In 2017 you have the power to tell your story to the world, and overall create many new opportunities for your future. Not only is it possible to transform your life in a short period of time, but by using social media you are able to:

1. Tell your story

2. Impact many people for the better

3. Help others

4. Connect with powerful individuals

    And more…

Now, you may be wondering how I was able to accomplish all of these life changing events in little over a year. Well, right now I will be giving you the secrets. In this chapter I will be giving you tips I've used to tell my story to thousands of people, and I will be teaching you about the value of a personal brand. Remember, building a personal brand is meant to help you by allowing you to get your message out, as well as create a culture around what you believe in. Plus, in today's society personal branding will help you in any social situation, as well as it'll create an online portfolio for you. This will build up your credibility in the marketplace, as well as open up many doors of opportunity.

Whether you have your own business or not, building a personal brand gives you leverage due to the fact that you have an audience. Building an audience of individuals who view you as an authentic individual will allow you to impact others. With this impact, you can carry it into whatever endeavour you get into in the future. Social media is only growing from here, and it's those individuals that start creating quality content who will reap the benefits.

What is a personal brand?

Many people get confused on the idea of a personal brand, and I am here to break it down in a simple form. A personal brand is YOU, and only YOUR STORY. As an individual you are able to create a personal brand around yourself to show people who you are, and overall express your story to them. A personal brand allows YOU to stand out from the thousands of people on social media, and it gives you so much leverage. For me, starting my personal brand on social media helped me gain clarity on my life, and helped me so much when I was in a negative place.

Not only is a personal brand important, but it is necessary in today's world. With the social media revolution happening so quickly, those who build authentic personal brands will be able to cultivate engaging audiences. Like I said before, a personal brand represents who you are, and what you stand for. Social media gives you the opportunity to represent yourself, and a personal brand allows you to showcase what you do, and who you are.

A personal brand is more than just your pictures of you, it's about how you make people feel when they view your social media pages. Whether it be you inspire them, make them laugh, view life in a different way, or give helpful tips, your personal brand should be focused on how you affect people when they view you on social media. By building an authentic perception of yourself on social media, you are able to tell your story, as well as impact many people all over the world.

Key Points of your personal brand

- *A personal brand is YOU*

- *A personal brand allows you to show your values*

- *A personal brand helps get your message out there*

- *A personal brand helps you gain clarity on your current situation*

- *A personal brand will build your confidence*

- *A personal brand will help you build connections*

Why is a personal brand helpful?

Over the last year I have been able to network with many multi millionaires, and even billionaires by building a personal brand on social media. By building a foundation on social media to represent who I am, it has allowed me to impact thousands of people online by telling my story. My story is very important to me because it separates me from everybody else when it comes to social media. By expressing your story on social media, you will be able to cultivate a group of individuals that your story has impacted. In life it all comes down to who are you impacting for the better, and with the power of social media you are able to reach many people. Maybe you aren't the type of individuals who sees yourself as a social media user, but you must open your eyes to the opportunity that awaits you. In order to start seeing massive changes in your life, you must start taking massive action. There in no growth in the comfort zone, and if you are looking for ways to change your situation start being comfortable with being uncomfortable. Develop a personal brand today and start putting out content on social media because so many opportunities will arise from it.

A personal brand is so helpful because it allows you to be YOU on social media. In a world filled with over 7 billion people, nobody has the same story as you, as well as nobody is YOU! You are an individual, and building a personal brand gives you the opportunity to separate yourself on social media. The way I like to look at a personal brand is like a virtual business card. Once you give your social media name to somebody, they can instantly see who you are based on the content you put out. People who come to your social media pages will cultivate an understanding of what you do based on what you post. You have absolute control of what you put on social media, and you must start thinking about how each and every piece of content correlates back to how you want people to view you on social media.

Meeting New Individuals Has Changed My Life

In the modern world you don't have to fly thousands of miles away to connect with somebody new. You have the ability of making life changing connections with people all over the world right at your fingertips. Over the last year I've had the ability to connect with many successful individuals by using social media. A lot of people underestimate the power of an authentic comment on somebody's picture, or a simple direct message. People use social media to connect with others, and you have the ability to connect with powerful individuals each and every single second. One thing I've learned about connecting with people on social media is that it all comes down to consistency.

For example, I wanted to connected with 15 year old Caleb Maddix (@calebmaddix). Caleb is a 15 year old entrepreneur who is somebody who absolutely changed the direction of my life. After following Caleb for months, and consistently trying to connect with him I was finally able to have a conversation with him. I was able to do that because I was constantly commenting on his pictures on Instagram telling him how much his content has affected my life, and that I would very much appreciate a quick conversation with him. Due to the fact I have been showcasing my journey on social media and telling my story, my page caught his attention. Also, during this time I had recently gotten interviewed on ABC Channel 8 news, and I talked about how Caleb had impacted my life. Once the interview was released on TV, I sent him the link to check it out and he was interested in what I was doing.

This connection I made with Caleb turned into a huge opportunity for me. Fast Forward a couple weeks, and he invited me out to San Diego, California to speak in front of an audience about my story, as well as what I've been able to accomplish. Simply by building a personal brand, I was able to get introduced to a life changing opportunity. At 16 years old, getting invited out to San Diego, California to speak about my story seemed like a dream. This opportunity instantly opened up my eyes to see what was possible by making new connections on social media. I highly advise you to start taking your personal brand serious because you never know what it will lead you into.

While I was in San Diego, California I attended the Epic Mastermind Experience. This is a three day event in which many game changers came together and shared their story, as well as dropped in depth strategies about business. During my time at this event, I was able to network with many people who I admire on social media. A few key individuals I connected with were people such as Jeremy Haynes, Dan Fleyshman, and Joshua Earp. All of these individuals were featured in a Tai Lopez course that I had recently invested in. While at the event I had no idea that networking with a diverse amount of people would lead into many new opportunities.

The day I got home from the Epic Mastermind Experience was a day that I will always remember. While sitting at my desk, I ran across a Tai Lopez video on Instagram and I took action on trying to connect with him. During this time in my life I was very pumped up due to the fact that I had just spoken at my first event, and I was able to meet many powerful individuals. When trying to connect with Tai, my end goal was to tell him my story, as well as tell him that I was able to connect with the individuals that were in his course. I spoke at the same event as his peers, and I was focused on informing Tai about this achievement. I started to comment on Tai's pictures trying to connect with him, even though he gets thousand of comments. After almost giving up, I sent Tai a very informative direct message about how he has changed my life with his 67 steps, as well as how it has led me to meeting such influential people. I told him my story about getting diagnosed with interspinous ligament damage, and I informed him about how I spoke at the same event as Jeremy Haynes, Dan Fleyshman, and Joshua Earp.

After waiting for about five minutes, I received a direct message back from Tai Lopez, and he asked me the question, "how old are you, and how has my program helped you". I was in shock because I was honestly not expecting a reply back. Then, I massaged Tai back telling him that I was 16 years old, and I explained to him how his courses have changed the direction of my life. The reply I got next was an absolute game changer. After Tai read my response, he replied, "You should come to Los Angeles to shoot a video with me". Once I read that message, I didn't know what to say. Tai ended up giving me his personal phone number, and we set up a date for me to come out to his house in Beverly Hills, California.

A Simple Direct Message

By simply direct messaging Tai Lopez and telling him my story, I was able to create a life changing opportunity for myself. As I was only 16 years old, Tai also flew my mom to Los Angeles with me. I was stoked about this opportunity because I was able to take my mom to a place she has never been before. This opened up my mom's eyes to the amount of opportunity in the world today, as well as gave her a memorable experience. During our time in Los Angeles we met many amazing individuals including Jaiden Gross, and Jose Aristimuno. Both of these individuals have seen massive success in Tai's social media marketing programs, and I was able to create a strong relationship with them.

The reason I am telling you this is because I want you to see the power of connecting with others on social media. You may not believe a huge social media influencer will respond back to you, but you must believe that anything is possible. Set no limitations on who you want to connect with, but rather go all in on making connections with influential individuals.

A personal brand is not only helpful, but it is NECESSARY if you are serious about changing your life, and getting introduced to many life changing opportunities.

Key Points

- *It will lead to new opportunities*

- *It will help you convey your story*

- *It will help you make new connections with powerful people*

With social media being a very powerful tool in this modern society, building a personal brand will allow you to be introduced to many new opportunities. Showcase your journey on social media, and focus on building a compelling brand story for your audience.

The Value of A Brand Story

When it comes to building a personal brand on social media, people want to see your story. Social media is so powerful because you can showcase your journey, and people can follow it along the way. One thing that I like to tell the people who I work with is, "if you can showcase yourself getting from point A to point B on social media, then you're worth following."

People connect to people, and if you want to start building an audience you must be the most authentic version of yourself. In order for you to create a "brand story" you must first understand what you want to convey to your audience. What I mean by that is what do you want your audience to know you as?

For me it was simple because my entire journey had started when I first got diagnosed with interspinous ligament damage. When I first began branding myself on social media, that was my focus. I wanted people to know me as the individual who had a severe neck injury, and how I was able to turn it into a positive outcome. That was the start of my story, but when it comes to building your brand story you must figure out how you want to convey yourself to your audience.

Your Perception On Social Media

The biggest mistake I see people make when branding themselves on social media is that they don't have a clear vision. When it comes to crafting content for your personal page, you must understand that social media contains millions of people. In order for your page to stand out, you must be completely authentic. There are so many Instagram accounts that look the same, or post the exact type of content. The value that comes with a personal brand is that it is YOU, and it stays with you forever.

If you are getting ready to finally start creating your personal brand, there are a few key questions I want you to ask yourself:

1. Where do I want to see myself in six months?

2. Based on my current situation, how can I convey myself on social media?

3. What three key points do I want to be known for?

4. How do I want people to view me when they come to my page?

These questions may seem simple, but they are the key points that will make or break your personal brand. It is very important that when you start creating content that you have a visual understanding of how you want people to view you. Each and every piece of content you put out all comes together to create an image of yourself that people know you as. Think about six months from now, and focus on where you want to be. Once you have a firm understanding on where you want to be in six months, you can start to get a feeling of what type of content you want to put on your page. It is very important to get crystal clear on your goals so that you have a clear understanding on where you want to be.

"Get clear on who you are, who you're not, and who you want to become."

-Peter Voodge

Now, I don't know the exact situation you may be in, but I do know that you have a way that you can tell your story on social media. Weather you are in a very negative situation, or at a peak in your career social media gives you so much leverage. Your story has the ability to impact other people's lives, and by using social media you can reach a huge market of individuals. Although there are millions of people on social media, the impact that your story can have on a single individual is remarkable.

When people come to your page on social media, you must have a page that instantly tells people who you are and what you do. A big factor that helps with this is having a compelling BIO. The first thing people see when they come to your page is your BIO, and from that they will decide if you are the type of person they want to follow.

5 Important Steps When Creating a Compelling BIO:

1. List what you do, or what you are passionate about

2. List your credibility factors (if any)

3. Give them a reason to follow (giveaways, prizes, etc.)

4. List your three pillars in which you want people to know you for

5. Be authentic, and tell who you are in a sentence

Having a compelling BIO will allow people to know what niche you are in, and immediately find out if you are somebody who they want to connect with. Your BIO will lead people into checking out the content on your page, but the biggest factor you must focus on is the content around your personal brand.

When I consult with individuals about personal branding, I always tell them to find their 3 pillars. Your 3 pillars are the three things that you want to be known for/stand out for. Once you find your 3 pillars for your brand story, then you must start to focus on building content that correlates to your pillars. Each piece of content you put on social media should correlate back to your pillars, so that you can focus on building the longevity of your personal brand.

How Do I Find My 3 Pillars?

Discovering your pillars is simple, and it all starts with understanding who you are. For example, if you are in a specific niche such as (E-Commerce, stocks, social media marketing, public speaking,etc.) then you must correlate that into your personal brand. If you are not into any specific industry, your pillars should be three values that make you who you are, and overall help you stand out from everybody else. Also, one of your pillars may be something you live by such as giving back to the community. Whatever you pick for you pillars, you must understand that you should post content that always correlates to them. This will start to make your social media page define who you truly are, and it will give people a better reason to follow you.

Key Points

- *Find your niche*

- *Figure out how you want to be conveyed on social media*

- *Be authentic / Be yourself*

Be sure to check out my Instagram BIO @caseyadams1 for examples of using pillars in your BIO.

Actionable Steps To Take:

1. Figure out your true values

2. Find at least 3 pillars for your personal brand

3. Adopt the mindset of using your personal brand to network

4. Constantly try to get in contact with people you want to connect with

5. Focus on each piece of content, and how it correlates to you

Growth Hacks on Social Media

In this section you are going to meet Tim Karsliyev who is the Founder of the verified page @DailyDose on Instagram. He has grown his page to over 1,100,000 followers in little over a year and a half, and runs one of the largest motivation, inspiration and business networks on Instagram.

He is going to answer a few questions about how he's been able to build such a huge movement, and how you can too. I've had the honor to ask him a few questions about growing an instagram as well as overcoming negativity. He talks about his negative moment, and how he was able to overcome them.

Tim Karsliyev

What has been the biggest setback in your life, and how did you overcome your tough situation?

The biggest setback I've had is not knowing the why... why am I doing what I'm doing. I believe the biggest setback anyone can have in life is not knowing why they are doing what they're doing. The way I overcame this is I took some time away from all the noise around the world to sit back and asked a question... Tim why are you doing this? This helped me have a clear understanding of my purpose. A person without a purpose is the only thing without a purpose on planet earth. If you just look around your living room or the porch or wherever you are right now everything around you has a purpose... and so should you.

What was the biggest breakthrough moment for you, and what was the most effective way you started building momentum in your life?

The biggest breakthrough I've had in my life was leaving my corporate lifestyle. It was right before the summer when everybody was getting ready to go out to the beaches, tan I was thinking about how I was going to make it. I just left my pay check behind. So meanwhile I had not been following my dread. I was spending half of my time in the corporate world, and the other half on building my dream. In times you have to take risk and not look back. Taking a risk and moving forward is what created the momentum in my life. You're only limitation is your imagination.

Can you give 3 practical tips on how the readers can turn their negative situation into a positive outcome?

Turning a negative into positive is part of being human because we only have one life to live. We have nothing to lose but everything to gain. Life is just a moment, max it out.

When it comes to building an engaged following on social media, what are 3 key points that the reader needs to know?

The most important thing about creating an engaged social media is investing time into your content. Make sure you impact people in a positive way, and create an emotional reaction.

Can you give the readers 3 tips on building an authentic personal brand on social media?

Take lots of pictures and make sure that they are high quality. Show people a glimpse of your life, family, and loved ones. Also, respond to every message you receive. It all starts with being personal to your audience and building a relationship with them.

Connect with Tim

Instagram: @DailyDose

Personal Instagram: @timkarsliyev

Remember, when it comes to putting out content you must create an authentic image of yourself that you want to convey to people. The start of your personal brand will lead to so many opportunities, and overall it will stay with you forever. No matter what business you are in, your personal brand stays with you. Once you start to leverage it, you will start to see many new opportunities for you and your business.

Once you have an understanding that you are the brand, you will start to develop a huge understanding behind the value it has on your future. In this time, social media gives you a platform to tell your story, and overall can help you create many new opportunities in your life.

Where To Start

Once you have an understanding of the 3 pillars that you want to convey yourself as, you must begin to put it into action. Many people get caught up "preparing to prepare" and they never take action... THAT CAN'T BE YOU. In order for you to start developing a unique personal brand, you must be 100% organic with your content. You can always delete content off your page, so the sooner you start the better.

Understand that your personal brand is all about showing where you are in your life at that current moment, so that as you continue to grow people have a story to follow. No matter what point you are at in your life or your business, document your journey and put out tons of quality content.

You can direct message me on Instagram @caseyadams1 for any questions, and we will talk about your personal brand more in depth. What got me so many opportunities over the last six months was by connecting with people on social media, and leveraging my personal brand. YOU CAN DO IT TO, but it's all up to you.

Go create content today because as you go along your journey you will see how much of a significant impact it can make on your life. It will allow you to connect with your followers on a personal level, and overall help you make an impact with your story. From building a personal brand on social media, I have been able to connect with many individuals who have changed the direction of my life. I will be going over the process I used to start networking with such influential individuals, and how you can as well.

Connecting With Powerful People On Social Media

Over the last year, I've been able to build many powerful connections on social media. For example, I've been able to connect with Caleb Maddix (@calebmaddix), Tai Lopez (@tailopez), Gerard Adams (@gerardadams), Ryan Blair (@realryanblair), Dan Fleyshman (@danfleyshman), Jeremy Haynes (@jeremy), Kevin Harrington (@realkevinharrington), and many more highly successful people. Out of the people that I have listed above, I have met the majority of them in person. By utilizing social media, I have been able to drastically grow my network, and overall I've been introduced to so many new opportunities. Now, many people have a social media, but not that many people are using it to build relationships with such influential people. Social media gives everybody the opportunity to be on the same platform, and it comes down to you to make that valuable connection. What I've learned over the past year is that it all comes down to you being genuinely interested in other people's content. Once people sense that you honestly want to connect with them, they are more likely to notice you. It all comes down to the first impression on social media, and I will be going over what I've done to connect with such influential people. This is a method that I've used to get interactions with people who I've wanted to connect with. You must stay consistent with everything you do when it comes to social media, and overall implement strategies that you believe will work best.

How To Connect With Influential People On Social Media

Now, I'm going to tell you what I've done to connect with such influential people on social media. First off, there is no "guarantee" with who you are going to get in contact with on social media, but I will be sharing with you a few tips that I have found success with. First off, let me explain the value that connecting with powerful people offers you. For me, connecting with successful individuals on social media has caused me to grow my network exponentially. Without social media, it would have been much harder to make connections with the people who I currently know. The people who I have listed above led me to speaking on stages with game changing entrepreneurs, as well as opened up many new opportunities for me. Once you learn how to properly connect with people on social media, you will start to realize how easy it is to connect with people who you admire. Remember, the people who you meet in the next year will determine the direction of your life, and you always want to focus on surrounding yourself with people who will push you forward. The people who you connect with on social media can have a direct correlation to what you are doing in the next year. I will be giving you tips on how I've been able to connect with such influential people on social media, and how you can to.

Appreciative Comments

Many people underestimate the power of a comment on social media, and do not see the value in it. I am here to talk to you about how leaving genuine comments on others posts will help you get closer to speaking with an individual who you want to speak with. Awhile back I wanted to get in contact with Gerard Adams on Instagram, but I knew he had so many messages. I decided to start commenting on each of his posts regarding how his content has impacted me. Yes, a lot of people comment on his posts, but I decided I had to stand out if I wanted to get in contact with him. On each post that Gerard started making, I began writing in depth comments regarding the impact that he has made on my life, and how important it would be for me if he got in contact with me. As he continued to put out content, I continued to leave valuable comments regarding how he has impacted my life. After a while Gerard started noticing me due to the fact I was being consistent with his content. One day he finally reached back out to me, and I got so excited. Due to the fact that I stayed consistent with his content, led me into being able to connect with him on social media. I was able to utilize my resources, and end up on a facetime call with Gerard. The facetime call that I had with Gerard changed my perspective about what I was doing, and it led me onto a new path in my life. He spoke with me about the value of mastering your craft, and from that day I've been a changed person. Also, I was able to meet Gerard at the Epic Mastermind Experience in San Diego, California. Overall, by leaving appreciative comments on other people's posts, you are given the opportunity to connect with many key individuals. The key to getting the attention of an influential individual is by being consistent with in detailed comments, and always making sure to tell them how much of an impact that they've made on your life. This principle allowed me to connect with one of my biggest mentors, and it all started by utilizing the comment section on Instagram. I challenge you to get on your phone right now, and go leave a long detailed comment on somebody's page who you'd like to meet one day.

Being Genuinely Interested In Somebody

Now, this strategy that I've used isn't a "copy & paste" type of strategy. In order for you to reach a certain individual, you must be genuinely interested in them. Being engaged in their content, and believing in their message is a huge advantage. When people start to read the comments that you leave, they will be able to tell if you are engaged in their content. As an individual you have to have a burning desire to connect with that individual, and you have to do it in a unique way. In order for you to get in contact with somebody who has a massive audience, you have to stand out and be consistent.

For me I would comment my entire story, and explain to them how their content has impacted me in a specific way. I would do this because at the end of the day people put out content to impact people. If you come off in an authentic way, and give them a meaningful message then you are more likely to be noticed by them. Now, you may ask yourself, "I don't want to annoy them," but you must break past that mental framework. If you honestly appreciate them, and their content has impacted you then give it your everything to get in contact with them. Be consistent with your message, and never get down on yourself if they do not respond. Everybody on social media has their own life in the real world, but you are able to get in contact with powerful people who can potentially make a huge difference in your life. The connections I've made on social media completely changed my situation, and I am so thankful for all of the new opportunities in my life. Reaching out to such influential people has opened up my eyes to the power of networking on social media, and has overall led me to many new opportunities. Remember, in order to increase the likelihood of connecting with somebody on social media, you must become genuinely interested in their content, and believe in their message.

CHAPTER 7

How Successful Entrepreneurs
Overcame Negativity

If you realized how powerful your thoughts are, you would never think a negative thought.

-Peace Pilgrim

A s a young entrepreneur, I've been able to meet some of the most humbling individuals on this planet. I've had the opportunity to speak with many multi millionaires, and even billionaires throughout my journey thus far. After speaking with many successful individuals, I have began to realize how each and every successful entrepreneur has dealt with adversity. All of the successful individuals who I have connected with have been through a life changing moment, and have had to deal with a lot of negativity. Those who become successful fail many times along the way, and the negative moments in their life shape who they are as an individual. No matter what your situation is right now, don't dwell on the negativity in your life. You must see the negativity as fuel for you to reach the next level in your life. In this chapter you will be getting introduced to many world class individuals, and they will be telling you their story of how they have dealt with negativity. Each and every one of these individuals has achieved massive success in their life, but they have also been through many terrible situations. Learn from those who have accomplished great things, and start implementing some of these strategies into your own life.

First, I want to introduce you to an individual that has had a huge impact on my life. His name is Gerard Adams, and he's helped me become a true leader. Gerard's story is very unique, and I am so grateful that I have the opportunity to feature him in my book.

Gerard Adams

Gerard Adams is an American serial entrepreneur, millennial branding expert, philanthropist, TEDx speaker and business executive. Adams is best known as co-founder of Elite Daily, which sold to the Daily Mail in 2015 for $50 million.

Facing Negativity:

There's real problems in the world, and somebody said to me recently, "you know what a real problem is? It's something that money can't fix." A lot of our problems that we face and complain about, money can fix. You must remember that when you have a problem that money can't fix, then that's a real problem. We must all be grateful for each and every day, and we must stay positive in our lives. A lot of people who have it way worse than you still continue to be happy everyday. If you start to develop that mentality, and mindset to push forward every day you will soon start to manifest so many things in your life. You manifest opportunity, and you have that law of attraction bring back positivity into your life. I truly believe that once you put this good energy into the world, it comes back to you.

There was once this time that I went snowboarding with a bunch of my friends, and they all took me back country. Believe it or not, at that moment I have never been snowboarding backcountry before, and I was scared. I told my friends, "guys I can't do this, I'm not that great." They believed in me, and we continued to take the route that I was not comfortable with taking. After a couple of minutes of going down the slopes, I started to slow down because I was not comfortable with the terrain. Lo and behold, they ended up moving to far ahead and completely lost me. The mountain we were snowboarding on was one of the biggest mountains in Wyoming. Now, all of the sudden it started getting dark out, I have no helmet, there's rocks and trees that I'm going through, I had to hike, and I was completely by myself. It was getting completely dark out, and it was freezing cold during this time. I had to figure out how I was going to get down this mountain because if I don't get down this mountain, I could die. Also, if I made a mistake and I fell and hit my head, then I would definitely die. I needed to be very careful, and figure out how I was going to make it down the mountain alive. I'll never forget what I then said to myself, and that was, "Gerard, this is adversity at it's finest, and you need to do whatever it takes to pull yourself together, be strong, be smart, and get to the bottom of this mountain." After hours of finding my way down this massive mountain, I finally found my way to the bottom. When I finally got to the bottom of that mountain, the rescue team said to me, "Gerard, you don't even know how many people die every weekend because of this. We couldn't find you, it was very dark, and you are very lucky."

As I look back, it's so crazy to me that stories like that have impacted me so much. There was a time when I almost drowned, and I also have a scar on my face that many people do not know about. This scar runs from my cheek to under my nose, and the story behind it has made a huge impact on my life. First off, I grew up in a town where I have gotten jumped, there was gangs, drugs, and all that type of stuff. One time, I was getting chased by a gang and I went to jump over a fence not knowing that there was sharp metal posts on top. As I approached the fence, I went to flip over the fence with a jiu jitsu move I had learned awhile back. As I was attempting this flip over the fence, my face gets stabbed by one of the point in my fence. My face was literally stuck on one of the poles, and my face started bleeding profusely. Lucky somebody saw what had just happened to me, and they came and helped me. I am so grateful for them because they ended up taking me to the hospital, and saving my life.

There has been so many moments like this in my life in which I've had to fight through adversity. Whether it was business, life threatening moments, or anything else I've been able to push through. No matter what, each and everyday I feel grateful because I am alive. I get to wake up every single day, and just live life. Every day is a canvas to just live and create, be passionate, and to be happy. You know weather I meet somebody who is a janitor, or a billionaire I treat them the same. You must start to adapt, and be that type of person. Be grateful, put out good energy, be positive, have faith, and believe in yourself. There is going to be those low moments in your life where you don't know if you are going to make it down that mountain. You must pick yourself up, you need to be strong, and you must know that it's all up to you to make it down "that mountain." In every aspect in your life, you must push yourself to those limits, and you will. Sometimes it's going to be you, and nobody else. This is when you must pick yourself up, and tell yourself, "you know what, this is adversity at it's finest. I'm strong, I'm positive, and I know I can do this," and then take action and do it. Those are the moments that are going to shape your life, and once you learn to deal with adversity at it's finest, you can accomplish anything.

I want you to take a moment right now to reflect on the story that Gerard just told you. The meaning behind his words are so powerful, and he is the true example of a leader. Following

Gerard's journey over the last year has helped me become the person who I am today. I had the opportunity to meet Gerard at an event in San Diego, California in which I was able to listen to his story first hand. Gerard is a true example of a leader and his story is impacting hundreds and thousands of individuals. Make you stay connected with what Gerard Adams is up to on social media.

Social Links:

www.GerardAdams.com

Instagram: @gerardadams

Twitter: @IAMgerardadams

The next guest I will be introducing you to is somebody who I admire greatly. His name is Jaiden Gross and I had the opportunity to meet him at Tai Lopez's house in Beverly Hills. When I had the opportunity to spend a weekend with Tai Lopez, Jaiden and I stayed at the hotel and were able to hang out for three days. We've built a strong relationship since then and today he will be sharing with you who he is and how he transformed his life.

Jaiden Gross

Description of who I am, and what I've accomplished:

My name is Jaiden Gross. I am a 21 year old serial entrepreneur renown as the #1 Social Media Marketing Agency success story of Tai Lopez's online eCourse. My rise to "fame," came of recent, back in December of 2016, after I had achieved a gross revenue of $32,600 in two months. This put me on projection to create a six-figure income for the coming year. Since then, I've grown my social media marketing agency to seven figures and have employed 40 team members across the globe, in over 6 countries. Our client base is made-up of primarily doctors; however, we've branched off into several other industries, including franchisees, restaurants and private equity firms, real estate developers and many more. Since mid-February of 2017, I have been live training fellow social media marketing agency students of the Tai Lopez eCourse and it grew from a handful of students, to over 200 individual sessions, with an elite monthly mastermind group of 50 hungry entrepreneurs. As I write this in late April of 2017, I am amidst many projects, one in particular I'm most excited to release: a Mobile Application that will revolutionize the face of sales training. Its expected date of release is undecided, however, goals of beta versions are set for July of 2017.

Q: What has been the biggest setback in your life, and how did you overcome your tough situation?

The biggest setback in life for me was when my parents informed me of their divorce. Although it's fairly common now, it didn't lighten the blow towards my 13 year old mind, body and spirit. I never "overcame," this burden per say, but I did come to terms with it and have accepted it. And this is an important statement I want to make clear. In life, there isn't always a cookie-cutter answer to your problem, and that's okay. Sometimes accepting what has happened and moving forward, IS the best answer. I remember trying to change their opinions on why they sought divorce, only to further disappoint myself. Dwelling in past expectations only ruin the joy of what opportunities lie in front of you, today.

Q: When you were dealing with negativity in your life, how did you turn your negative situation into a positive outcome?

At first, in very unhealthy ways. I escaped with drugs early on in high school, succumbing to peer pressure. That further progressed to surrounding myself with the wrong people, malnourishing myself, negative self-talk, bullying others, and lastly pure isolation from those who cared. Eventually, as the saying goes, "you'll hit your own rock bottom". I did. I was broken emotionally, financially, spiritually and physically and refused to let the rest of my life become shambled to what was the present. I looked towards the future and clearly defined where I was to be in 5 years. What kind of house I wanted. What type of car I drove. And then I did the math. One of my favorite quotes I live by is from Warren Buffet, who says, "For anything you want in life, do the math." This resonates with me on many personal levels, as numbers provide assurance towards certainty. I wrote down 10 goals, every single day. As cliché as it sounds, this daily ritual is often the most powerful way to turn a negative situation into gratefulness.

Q: What was the biggest breakthrough moment for you, and what was the most effective way you started building momentum in your life?

The breakthrough moment in life happened when I was 18 years old and I had been working at a sales job for a large consulting firm. I had realized that I was working harder, smarter and longer, than the people who worked above me, and cared more about the people I brought to them than they did. It was at that very moment I knew I was to be an entrepreneur. It made it very difficult for me to think about working for someone else again and after that, I began experimenting with entrepreneurial ventures. The sure fire way to build effective momentum for yourself in life is just to provide more and more and more for the world that stands before you. Eventually, someone will become attracted to what you are doing. It is at that very moment where you must decide your purpose. If you feel your purpose is against what others are attracted to, you're playing for the short-term. Always stride towards the long-haul and never stop until you find that one thing that fulfils you.

Q: Can you give 3 practical tips on how the readers can turn their negative situation into a positive outcome?

#1 – Count on yourself. An empty cup cannot fill another and you must always remember that. Plus, you need to tell yourself that you're the best, no matter what. Seek courage from within, not through others. There will be times where others wish to take advantage of your good nature and this can become destructive towards your success. You'll become a "Doormat" and others will think less of you, as you never set a standard for yourself.

#2 – Learn something new every single day. I personally spend a minimum of 2-3 hours reading every single day to further improve myself. You must think of your mind as an engine. Every day it requires fuel and knowledge is the highest grade. If reading is not your forte, listen to audio books or watch videos. In the 21st century, A.K.A. the information era, there's no reason why you cannot learn anything you set your mind to.

#3 – Give first, second, third, then request something in return. People are like bank accounts; before you can withdraw on them, you must first deposit something of value to them. No one likes to have their relationship go back to square one, so therefore, you must never seek equality in exchange. Always seek to provide more than what's required of you and the right people will do the same for you. This is what will create harmonious relationships.

Q: What is the most practical advice you can give somebody reading my book who is in a negative situation or stuck in a place they don't want to be?

Don't be a reader of your own story, become the storyteller. You write your own story and so you can always re-write, time after time again. So often I'll hear from younger entrepreneurs how a negative situation happened "TO THEM," versus because of them. If you believe yourself a victim of circumstance, entrepreneurship is not the path for you. It is a winding, dangerous and uncertain road that breeds fear in those who live life by the book. There is no "right" or "wrong" in entrepreneurship, only what is most effective and most efficient. Focus on what solutions you can bring to tomorrow and you'll be better off today then you've ever been.

Stay Connected With Jaiden Gross

Instagram: @grossjaiden

Snapchat: Altrui

Facebook: Jaiden Gross

LinkedIn: Jaiden Gross

Up next I want to introduce you to somebody who is absolutely crushing it in their industry. His name is Jeremy Haynes and I had the opportunity to connect with him in San Diego, California as well. After hearing Jeremy's story, I instantly knew that I wanted him to provide value in my book. He has faced many negative situations in his life, but today he will be sharing with you his story and how he has overcome negativity in his life.

Jeremy Haynes

Who Is Jeremy Haynes?

Currently I am building the most elite, go-to personality brand digital agency that celebrity personalities, entrepreneurs and business people alike with real results, come to when they want to become well-known experts while generating massive revenues in the process.

My agency drives high impact results for each of our clients, by disseminating content and other lines of communication to bring attention to the personality and then we monetize that attention, with information products that are both tangible and intangible.

I've been able to take this path in life with passion and experience from my background starting as an entrepreneur at age 16, and working under mentors like Grant Cardone as his digital marketing specialist for over 13 months. I was able to help take Grant's digital revenues from $40,000 monthly to over $1.8M monthly with the help of the creative team, sales team and of course--Grant.

Since starting my current agency Megalodon Marketing and narrowing our speciality to Personality Brand Development, we've worked with some of the largest personalities that disseminate information products. It's what we do.

What has been the biggest setback in your life, and how did you overcome your tough situation?

One of my largest setbacks in life came from was when I first moved to Miami, at age 19 with only $125 in my pocket. I had climbed from a cell phone sales rep inside of Costco in North Miami Beach to the Head of Marketing for an LED distribution franchising company out of North Miami. I was gifted with this opportunity after presenting the best version of myself to a gentleman named Peter, who I had sold a phone too.

Sometimes you ask for advice and get a check, and that is what I learned that day. I asked him as a successful business person for mentorship with a business I was trying to launch at the time and he instead hired me.

After working for him for only 3 months, he came to me one day after not paying me my weekly paycheck and informed me his company had failed--and he had to let me go. I was devastated, but not defeated! The only thing I know to do when I'm in trouble like that is take action to get out of the trouble. Move forward was my motto.

I put my updated resume with my recent Head of Marketing title added to it on Indeed.com and 3 days later, as a half scared but excited for opportunity 19 year old, received a call from Grant Cardone's recruiting agency who sought me out for a job opportunity. They hired me as a temp to train their sales team to efficiently use infusionsoft and to send emails to their, at the time 150,000 person database.

At the end of my 13 months of working for him and leaving with the title of Digital Marketing Specialist, growing the database to 450,000+ and driving millions in revenues, I left to start my agency with the confidence coming from the results I was able to generate for Grant. Hope is not a strategy but it helps ease your nerves.

When you were dealing with negativity in your life, how did you turn your negative situation into a positive outcome?

I grew up in Ohio from 0 to 18 and hated every second of it. Everything about the state was negative including my conditioned perspective, at the time. The people, places, environment, conversations and mentality was limited and clouded with limited judgement and negativity. I never fit into that mindset and set of parameters to operate in though.

At age 16 I watched a Tony Robbins video on "How To Build Self Confidence," and it thankfully opened my mind and shifted my perspective. I started a business with my newfound confidence, as well as that, I had a set of videos I could turn to that would help me build my entrepreneur strategy.

At the time, I didn't know what I didn't know, I just knew I wanted to sell to make enough money to leave Ohio. In under 4 months, I generated over $60,000 in revenue with my video production company, HaynesFilms and then tanked it months later from not knowing how to run a business.

However, this accomplishment validated my perspective that I didn't fit in where I was at the time and 2 years later enabled me to leave Ohio and move to Denver at 18 to start my new life.

What was the biggest breakthrough moment for you, and what was the most effective way you started building momentum in your life?

One of my biggest breakthrough moments was when Greg S Reid--a current mentor told me to work on my business and not in my business at his #1 rated entrepreneur event--Secret Knock. From that moment onward I became an executive to my business and not a slave to the business day to day that was holding me and my perspective back unknowingly.

This moment forever enabled me to seek out education and council in areas of my life where I was activity focusing. I began to surround myself with others that could cover my blind spots to help me grow and overcome areas where I didn't know what I didn't know that could make me get much better.

My peak lift and ultimate surges of momentum comes from after speaking at a mastermind, hosting a mastermind or attending a mastermind. I've never obtained more momentum from an experience compared to a mastermind event.

Can you give 3 practical tips on how the readers can turn their negative situation into a positive outcome?

Your mentality is your greatest ally or your greatest enemy. Learn to control yourself physically, mentally and spiritually to flourish and prosper on all levels. Seek out knowledge in areas where you don't know what you don't know, but may be able to find something that can drastically improve your outcome after you've found it. And more importantly compared to anything else, apply the knowledge and lessons learned today into your tomorrows.

What is the most practical advice you can give somebody reading my book who is in a negative situation, or stuck in a place they don't want to be?

Somebody who's stuck or in a state of negativity may not even be able to hear or comprehend what I'm going to say as they are not in the right frame of mind for it.

You see, a majority of those that feel stuck, or are negative and can't rewire their brain simply don't want to. They are comfortable and ok with where they are, who they are and even though it may seem they aren't ok with their current circumstances--they are!

When an individual has enough will and personal leverage, they will use that to find the resources and what they need to overcome any situation, period.

I remember being at what felt like my lowest point in a 600 sq ft apartment with a shitty roommate next to the projects sitting on suitcases and sleeping on airbeds for the first 3 months I came to Miami. I remember every single day I would go to drive my 96 Toyota Camry that I'd have to put power steering fluid in EVERY DAY to drive to Costco to sell phones. I remember having to constantly push myself through it, I constantly had to sell myself that things would get better, but I always resonated with the reality that I would be the only one that could get myself out of those circumstances.

I remember having to be above myself, in times where I couldn't eat from not having money and my airbed popping again with no money to replace it. It sucked!

But guess what, I'm not there anymore! I managed to get out! My greatest asset was me! You have to take responsibility and accountability that if you're fed up, you need to use that and apply it into your life as personal leverage in order to improve your circumstances. And no matter, no matter how hard life becomes--you need to keep pushing and condition yourself to see positivity in everything going on. See and acknowledge the progress, embrace it wherever you can.

All in all, whoever you are and whatever you do--you can control more and generate more results for yourself if you apply a concentrated focus to that area of yourself. Never give up and always keep your eye on the up side, but never ignore the reality, just choose not to dwell in it. Become the next best version of yourself today, now is the best time to take action on your ideas and dreams.

Social Links

Company: www.megalodonmarketing.net/

Instagram: @Jeremy

FaceBook.com/TheJeremyHaynes

After hearing Jeremy's story, I know that you are pumped up. Once I came to the realization that every successful individual has dealt with negativity, it opened my eyes up to my current situation. I was at a very negative point in my life when I got diagnosed with interspinous ligament, but as I've continued to meet highly successful people I've came to the conclusion that progress is the only answer. Once you come across a negative time in your life, you must understand that the only way for you to go is forward. Implement what these individuals are saying and take action so you can reach your desired outcome.

Next, I will be introducing you to an individual named Myke Metzger. Me and Myke live in the same area near Richmond, Virginia and we connected by using social media. He's taught me many important skills and I am thankful that he has allowed me to share his story with you. After hearing Myke's story, I knew that so many people could find value from it. Make sure to stay connected with Myke on social media and continue to follow his journey.

Myke Metzger

What has been the biggest setback in your life, and how did you overcome your tough situation?

One of my biggest setbacks in life was truly myself. From the age of 18 through 24 I had created a life full of terrible habits which reflected the situation I was in during those years. I was constantly chasing girls, getting drunk and wasting all of my money. My parents were not too proud of me and I had become a result of the people I had chosen to surround myself with. Breaking out of this cycle was the most difficult thing I have ever experienced. It takes a massive amount of self awareness and desire to be able to change the direction in which your life is headed. I was sick and tired of being sick and tired and I knew something had to change if I didn't want to end up in jail or dead.

When you were dealing with negativity in your life, how did you turn your negative situation into a positive outcome?

The first thing that ever changed my mindset and helped me focus on the positive in life, was a book I read by Rhonda Byrne titled "The Power". I actually read this book during a weekend jail session that I had to complete after receiving my 4th "driving on a suspended license ticket".

The book changed my life forever, just like this one could change yours. From that moment on I decided I was going to take my circumstances under control and dictate my own thoughts. Your thoughts are what determine your reality and I have found that to be a fact. My best advice for you is to become self aware, and open your mind to new information that could change your thought process in a positive way. It may be from reading a book or watching a video, but all it takes is that first positive thought to create a chain reaction.

What was the biggest breakthrough moment for you, and what was the most effective way you started building momentum in your life?

My biggest breakthrough moment in my life was when I finally stopped trying to "gather more information" and I made the decision to truly take action. I forced myself to do the things that were maybe a bit uncomfortable, such as making that sales call that I had been avoiding.

A good example of an effective way I accomplished this is by having the confidence to speak to everyone I crossed paths with. If I entered an elevator with somebody in it, I would force myself to make eye contact and say hello and ask how their day was going. In the past, I would have never done that. I had to force myself out of my comfort zone and I encourage you to do the same.

Can you give 3 practical tips on how the readers can turn their negative situation into a positive outcome?

- *STOP "Getting Ready to Get Ready"*

  Most of the entrepreneurs that I know of who have been stuck for the past 3 years are still doing the same thing that they have been doing from the beginning...

PLANNING.

Stop planning and start doing. It is easy to distract yourself with social media and make motivational "quote memes" all day, but it produces zero results. Cut out all of the "fluff" and take action on what you already know needs to be done.

- *STOP Saying "Yes" To Every Opportunity*

  During your lifetime as an entrepreneur, you will have many "new opportunities" thrown at you. The commonalities that I have found throughout the people that fail, is that they willingly and eagerly say "yes" to all of them.

  As exciting and tempting as these opportunities may seem or sound, you must have the self control as a business person and a leader to say no. If you spread yourself too thin, you're useless to the people you're leading. Decide to become the master of one, instead of the jack of all.

- *STOP Trying To Avoid "Selling"*

  The backbone and foundation of any true success story is being able to sell. Whether it's the true story known as "The Pursuit of Happyness" (Will Smith 2006) or a panel of "sharks" on the investor series Shark Tank - sales is the motto.

  When investors are looking at a business, they are interested in the marketability of a product and if the figurehead of the product or company can actually SELL them on a vision. If you cannot sell, you're headed for a dead end.

The best of the best have mastered sales in all aspects of their life. Whether it's the skill of winning over new friends and influencing people, or myself simply selling to over 10,000 people from stage - sales is the key to winning big as an entrepreneur.

What is the most practical advice you can give somebody reading my book who is in a negative situation, or stuck in a place they don't want to be?

My most practical advice is not something you can touch or feel. It is not even something you can read or watch. It must start from within and if you cannot imagine success for yourself then it can never become a reality. I urge you to begin imagining yourself as a success story and when you can do that - it will slowly but surely begin to happen for yourself. Thoughts truly do become real things. Keep this in mind, and I wish you luck in your endeavour, towards definite success!

Social Links:

Website: www.MykeMetzger.com

Instagram: @mykemetzger

FaceBook.com/themykemetzgernetwork

Brad Cameron

Up next I'm going to be introducing you to Brad Cameron who is 24 from Melbourne, Australia. He is the owner of @buildyourempire on Instagram, a community of over 1 million entrepreneurs. He also has a free digital magazine "Build Your Empire Magazine" in the iTunes and Google Play store for entrepreneurs.

He has a free ebook coming out soon called **200 successful entrepreneurs answer "What is your best piece of advice that you can pass on to someone that wants to be an entrepreneur?"** that he is planning to impact as many people as possible with.

Soon he's releasing a watch brand that he has co-founded. To keep updated on this watch brand, feel free to follow @empire_timepieces on Instagram.

He's also aiming to leverage his Instagram page and magazine to raise $25,000 USD to build a school in Laos for kids in need via a Pencils of Promise campaign.

Now, I am excited to introduce you to the man himself Brad Cameron. I've asked him a few questions regarding how he has overcome negativity in his life. Remember, learn from those who are crushing it and you will take massive action.

What has been the biggest setback in your life, and how did you overcome your tough situation?

I've been fortunate enough to have no real massive setbacks in my life. But a setback that I didn't see coming was the breakup of a 3 year relationship. It was tough at first, but I overcame it by putting in the time into focusing on becoming a better person and learning the lessons from my mistakes from this relationship.

When you were dealing with negativity in your life, how did you turn your negative situation into a positive outcome?

By taking action to work on myself, my business and immerse myself into my hobbies. Sitting around at home would just lead to a negative mindset, and I'm most positive when I'm productive getting things done.

What was the biggest breakthrough moment for you, and what was the most effective way you started building momentum in your life?

Once again, I think the most effective way to start building momentum is to take massive action towards your goals. Results will start happening and if you keep taking that massive directed action it will all snowball into momentum in time.

Can you give 3 practical tips on how the readers can turn their negative situation into a positive outcome?

1. *Make it a habit to take responsibility for yourself and your situation and don't blame your problems on your environment thinking that you can't do anything about it.*

2. *Learn from the negative situation. Such as "How can I avoid getting into this situation next time?", "What can I do to improve myself from this?" etc.*

3. *Write down 3 things that can be a potential opportunity or positive outcome from ending up in this situation, and take massive action to work towards achieving those outcomes/opportunities.*

What is the most practical advice you can give somebody reading my book who is in a negative situation, or stuck in a place they don't want to be?

It's going to get better in time, most perceived problems in your life happening right now won't matter at all in 5 years from now.

Where can people find you on social media?

Instagram: @bradcameron_

The next person I want to introduce you to is somebody who I've had the opportunity to meet at an event I spoke at in San Diego, California. His name is Calvin Wayman and he's overcame a lot of negativity to get to where he is today. He's been able to quit his job and become a full time entrepreneur. Also, he has written a book called "Fish Out Of Water". Make sure you follow his journey and listen to what he has to say below.

Calvin Wayman

What has been the biggest setback in your life, and how did you overcome your tough situation?

One of my biggest setbacks was when I quit my day job to pursue my dream of being an entrepreneur. But after I quit my job, I didn't know exactly what I was going to do. I had a wife and a one-year old. I didn't know how I was going to support them. I was worried if I made the wrong decision because if I did then it would ruin everything.

I worried so much and built up so much anxiety, I was getting no more than 2 hours of sleep a night. I remember my wife waking me up because I was soaking HER with my sweat from stressing so much. I fell into a deep depression that was so low I ended up losing 10 pounds in less than a week!

Ultimately, how I got out of this tough situation is I realized I was in control of my own life and I had to make a decision and TRUST the decision. Through the process I learned that instead of worrying if it's the right decision, I realized it was up to me to make it right. That was a major key: successful people don't worry if they make a right decision or not. Instead, they make a decision and then they make it right.

I then started taking boatloads of action in the direction of my decision, and even though it was rocking, it all worked out.

When you were dealing with negativity in your life, how did you turn your negative situation into a positive outcome?

When dealing with negative situations, always ask "what's the good in this?" I've learned that in life, often times it's not really the situation that makes something "good" or "bad." We are the ones that make it good or bad, based on how we choose to see it.

I remember about a year ago, I was at an event near Phoenix, Arizona. I was driving late at night, and it was raining. I was one turn away from being to my destination. I turned on my right blinker, and went into the right turn-lane--only it actually WASN'T a turn-lane. It was a freaking sidewalk! Because it was dark and raining, and I couldn't tell! I ended up driving right into the curb and instantly BLOWING my car tire!

In this "negative" situation, I honestly was upset. I was so mad at myself for letting it happen. But then I asked the question, "whats' the good in this?" The good was, I got to my destination safely. The good was, my insurance would have someone come put on the spare tire and I wouldn't even have to worry about it. And most importantly, the good was that I was okay. Understanding the good, changed my whole perspective and I went to bed peaceful that night.

Then when I took the car into the car shop to get replaced the mechanic told me that my front brakes on my car have been wearing out so badly, that they were almost not going to work! "We are going to replace these brakes," he said. "I can't believe these brakes are working now. It's a good thing you came in today."

You just never know why something is happening. But how you feel about it is up to you. Always ask, "What's the good in this?"

What was the biggest breakthrough moment for you, and what was the most effective way you started building momentum in your life?

A MASSIVE breakthrough moment for me was almost two years ago, while I was doing door-to-door sales selling solar panels. I usually would get a sale every day, but then I went not 1, not 2, or even 3 days without a sale. I went 7 days! I was freaking out and wondering if I should quit.

Then that day, I went to an old man's house named Frank. He ended up buying! I was so excited that I finally got one! Part of the process after someone agreed to do it, is to get a "credit check" over the phone. I called the credit check person, gave them all of Frank's information, then I handed Frank the phone to just confirm his address and everything.

But what Frank did next surprised me and devastated me! Frank told the person on the phone, "You know what, I don't want to do a credit check.

Cancel everything!" And just like that, Frank cancelled the order. He handed me the phone and said, "sorry dude."

I was so discouraged, I was about to leave. I was like, "this is too negative! I don't know if I can take this!" But I realized that if I left, I would have ZERO chance of getting a sale. So I went back to the neighborhood and knocked doors all day until it was dark and I had to leave. But when I was leaving the neighborhood that day, I did something that changed my life forever. While I was angry, depressed, and worried that I just went 7 days with nothing, something came to me that said "Go back to Frank's house." It was dark. I randomly went back to Frank's house, unsure why I was even there. I rang the door-bell. After a few seconds, Frank opens the door. "Frank..." I said softly, "why don't you just...do this?"

Frank smiled! He said "You know what Calvin! I'm going to do it!" I was shocked! I couldn't believe what I was hearing. He then said, "I'm going to do it and I'll tell you why. It has nothing to do with that credit check anymore. It doesn't even have anything to do with the money I'm going to save on solar. I'm going to do it, and it's BECAUSE OF YOU." After a pause, he continued. "Look, I'm an older guy. I've been around a time or two. And I know that the people that succeed in life are the ones that don't quit and never give up. And because you didn't quit, because you came back, I'm going to give you the order." I was so overwhelmed with gratitude I didn't know what to say. Frank then put his hand on my shoulder and said with a smile, "Calvin, I know you're working hard. But don't quit. Keep going. Never give up."

That day changed my life forever. It was a massive breakthrough moment for me. And it developed something in me to never quit no matter what. That has created a GREAT momentum that still continues today.

Can you give 3 practical tips on how the readers can turn their negative situation into a positive outcome?

Always ask, "what's the good in this?"

Find out what's inside your control, and focus on that! Don't focus on what's outside your control.

Become a member of the CIA--take Consistent Imperfect Action. When you find yourself in a negative situation, just take an action, even if you're not sure if it's the right one. And it doesn't have to be perfect either. Just take a step. Take an action. Realize that "done" is better than "perfect."

What is the most practical advice you can give somebody reading my book who is in a negative situation, or stuck in a place they don't want to be?

Ask, where would you be in your life if you could be anywhere? What would you be doing? What kind of life do you want to have that's different than this? Once you know where you'd want to be, take one little small action in that direction. Over time, you'll get unstuck and find yourself living an amazing life.

How is social media important to you, and how has it affected your life?

Social media is a way to share with the world who you really, authentically are. Social media has changed my life in a major way. I've been blessed with a community of people that like me for who I am, and support me in everything I do. I wouldn't be able to have that without social media.

Stay connected with Calvin:

calvinwayman.com

Facebook.com/calvinwayman

Instagram: @calvinwayman

Snapchat.com/add/calvinwayman

Social media gives you and me the power to network with people all over the world, as well as in our communities. The next guest you may already know due to his viral videos on YouTube. His name is Jeff, and he is the owner of the "JR GARAGE" and "JR BUSINESS" YouTube channels. He has over a combined 600,000+ subscribers, and 40+ million combined page views. I was able to connect with Jeff over Instagram due to one of his team members named Kieran. Little did I know that he was only about an hour and a half away from where I live and absolutely crushing it. At just 17 years old, Jeff has started many successful 7 figure businesses, and he's here today to provide you guys with massive value!

JR GARAGE

Ever since I could walk and talk I have had a passion for business and entrepreneurship. When I was just 6 years old, my brothers and I decided to launch our lemonade stand in hopes of making some money. This was our first taste at business and it ultimately taught us quite a bit about the fundamentals of business, while making a few thousand dollars. In addition, we did virtually every single thing little kids could do to make a buck at the time. A few years later, we realized we had a passion for collecting vintage items. After buying some of our first collectables and later reselling them for a profit, we decided to launch our investment business in 2008. Since 2008, we have scaled this business to the point now where we supply thousands of investors across the world with rare collectables. Over the past few years, we have expanded and diversified our businesses in order to introduce many additional revenue streams. We have devoted the last 9 years of our lives to growing these various businesses into the seven figure empire they are today.

What has been the biggest setback in your life, and how did you overcome your tough situation?

Two major challenges we faced early on was being extremely young and flat broke. However, we were able to turn both of these "setbacks" into advantages. When the recession rolled around, my family faced numerous challenges. In simple terms, we were hundreds of thousands of dollars in debt and had virtually no income.

Because there was no money floating around the family, my brothers and I learned the value of a dollar extremely quickly. Our family didn't eat out, we never went to the movies, we didn't buy new clothes, etc. I always say having no money is what made me money. Had we not gone through the tough times, we would never have had the drive to succeed on the same level. Being extremely young was also a challenge for us at times. I was 9 years old when we entered the numismatic and collectible industry dominated by 40-70 year olds. People simply did not take us seriously. Sometimes, we were flat out ignored when we tried to do business. As a result, we matured very fast. We were told we were too young and didn't have enough money to succeed in business. We used this opposition as fuel to prove those people wrong. To this day, when haters hate on us, we use them as motivation to work even harder. "Haters are nobodies going nowhere, you are somebody going somewhere," is a quote of mine I like to tell people.

How did JR GARAGE start and what were your intentions with the YouTube channel?

Within the last year or so, we launched the YouTube channels JR Garage and JR Business. These YouTube channels are where we share our passion for cars and business respectively. They now have a combined 600,000+ subscriber following and 40+ million combined page views. What started as just a fun little place to share our passion with random people around the world, has now turned into something beyond our wildest dreams. We have been blessed with the ability to inspire and motivate others to succeed in life. While it does take a lot of time and energy to run these channels, the reward of seeing people benefit from our work is priceless.

What is the most practical advice you can give somebody reading my book who is in a negative situation, or stuck in a place they don't want to be?

I receive hundreds of messages from people who are "stuck" and need some advice to get going. While each case it different, I generally like to tell people to find your passion and find a way to make money with it. In this day and age, there are endless ways to make money, you just have to be creative. Use your creativity to find a niche and innovate. Once you find your niche, learn as much as you can. Learn from mentors in the industry! We have been fortunate enough to learn from dozens of knowledgeable experts over the years. Networking with other successful people in your industry is also a vital way to establish a strong footing moving forward. However, nothing will work if you don't work. Putting in the effort 24/7 is what makes success possible.

How is social media important to you, and how has it affected your life?

Social media is a vital aspect of our personal brand. I love having the ability to reach thousands of people within minutes with a simple Snapchat or Instagram post. Being able to interact with fans is awesome. It's fun to just take a break and talk with people. But not only is it fun, it can be a business. I have worked with companies to feature products on my social media platforms, and structured compensation in multiple ways including payment or an affiliate share of sales driven.

A Message From JR GARAGE:

The entrepreneurial lifestyle is something I wouldn't trade for anything. There is no limit on what you can do or how much money you can make. It doesn't matter where you come from, whether you are rich or poor, male or female, young or old; anyone has the opportunity to succeed as an entrepreneur. After just 17 years of living on this extraordinary planet, I have been able to experience so much, travel to so many places, and inspire millions of people at the same time!

Connect with JR GARAGE:

www.youtube.com/jrgarage/

www.youtube.com/jrbusiness/

Instagram: @jrgarageyoutube

Instagram: @teamjrbusiness

Through the course of this chapter, I hoped you gained massive insight from many successful entrepreneurs. All of these individuals have one thing in common, and that is that they never gave up. See, when it comes to entrepreneurship you are in full control. As you read stories from all of these successful entrepreneurs, you got to see the struggles that they went through. Each and every one of the individuals in this chapter has been through massive negativity, but they were able to turn their situation into a positive outcome.

Make sure you reach out to each and every one of the individuals listed in this chapter because they are willing to help you. A simple connection on social media is all it takes. Prior to reading this chapter, I personally would advise you to go study each individual who was featured because they are absolute game changers. Study the content they put on social media, as well as how they've been able to cultivate such massive movements.

Make sure to review this chapter due to the fact that there was many golden nuggets. Also, when you reach out to these individuals tell them about how their story from "Rise of The Young" has impacted you. Remember what Gerard Adams told you about facing adversity, *"you know what, this is adversity at it's finest. I'm strong, I'm positive, and I know I can do this"*. You must take what Gerard says, and implement it when you are facing negativity. Focus on developing a positive mindset in every situation, and you will see massive changes in your outcome.

CHAPTER 8

Connecting The Dots

Many people limit themselves from change due to the fact that they don't like being uncomfortable. They let negativity overrule them and their chance at success is very minimal. In order for you to start overcoming a negative situation, you must have a strong belief in the direction of your future. My journey thus far has consisted of a very negative shift in my life, and it was the overall pivoting point for me. You must discover your transition and create the opportunities that await you in your life.

At the beginning of the book I talked about being diagnosed with interspinous ligament damage. As I look back on my injury I see how I was able to utilize this negativity and use it as fuel to achieving new opportunities.

The vision I had from the beginning was not as crystal clear as I would have wanted it to be, but as I look back I see how each and every move I made led me in the right direction. Taking instant action is the determining factor for new opportunities. The action you take today will result in a different outcome than if you take action in five years.

Opportunity awaits each and every one of us, but it only comes to those who put themselves out there. You as an individual are the only thing holding you back from your full potential. Whether it be in business, relationships, athletics, or anything else, you have absolute control of your effort and the action you take.

When I was stuck in my neck brace I had so much despair in my life. I didn't know what I wanted to do, but I knew it was up to me to turn it around. Dealing with negativity will put you in a position to exceed your limitations, and break through your current situation. Opening my eyes to the power of looking backwards was something that I never realized was so true. Each and every action I've taken from being in my neck brace has led me to where I am today. I've been able to cultivate my story into a well known brand and by using the power of social media I've been able to reach a large group of people. Now it's time to tell your story and start drawing the lines. Each and every action you take will be a building block of new opportunity. Looking forward you may not see how one opportunity will lead to the next, but you will begin to see opportunities arise. By taking consistent action, you'll see how much opportunity has been waiting for you all along. It's critical to stop being comfortable with your current situation because there is no extreme growth in the comfort zone. Reach for new heights, and invest in every opportunity you get. Investing to meet people has been a game changer for me, in that I've been able to greatly increase my network. Start going out of your way to connect with others in your community who are like minded. Simply making a connection on social media with another individual had the ability to change the direction of your life. In chapter 6 I talked a lot about the value of a simple connection on social media, and how valuable it can be. A lot of people "know" the value of social media, but aren't properly taking action with the platforms that are given to us. Remember, focus on building relationships on social media because those who you connect with will guide you along your journey. You can become connected with next level game changers, and with consistent action you'll create the opportunity to connect with them on a personal level. The connections you make today will have a huge impact on where you are tomorrow. It's time for you to make a change and go get what you deserve.

Dealing with a negative situation in my life had been the turning point for me, as well as it can be for you. Negativity can either pull you down and keep you there, or be the transformation you've been needing all along. Once you are at your lowest point, you have the ability to think positive. Your outcome is based on the actions you take and the actions you take are based on the mindset you have. Therefore, once you have absolute control of your mind, you have absolute control of your life.

"If you are positive, you'll see opportunities instead of obstacles."
— Widad Akrawi

It's time for you to turn your mess into your message and create an impact on people from all over the world. One of the best ways for you to overcome negativity, is by doing something good for somebody else. Social media gives you the power to cultivate your story, and impact people from all over the globe. Your message is so important because somebody out there in the world can value from it. Furthermore, you can inspire people with your message and start creating a massive impact on others. In order for you to start seeing changes in your life, you must be the change. Start investing in opportunities, building a movement on social media, telling your story and impacting people. Reading this book isn't going to be the transformation in your life, but what you implement into your daily routine will be the pivotal point. It's time for you to find your purpose and take action on new opportunities. Turning your negative situation into a positive outcome all starts with you and it's time to take action.

Made in the USA
Middletown, DE
24 July 2017